UNEXPECTED
MIRACLES

How sweet the moonlight sleeps upon this bank!
Here will we sit and let the sounds of music
Creep in our ears; soft stillness and the night
Become the touches of sweet harmony.
Sit, Jessica. Look how the floor of heaven
Is thick inlaid with patens of bright gold.
There's not the smallest orb which thou behold'st
But in his motion like an angel sings,
Still quiring to the young-eyed cherubims;
Such harmony is in immortal souls,
But whilst this muddy vesture of decay
Doth grossly close it in, we cannot hear it.

—Shakespeare, *The Merchant of Venice*

CONTENTS

PROLOGUE

Synchronicity takes the events in space and time as meaning
more than mere chance.
— Carl Jung

Synchronicity happens when something fateful is afoot. It may
not be just coincidence that you are reading this book. It may be
a just coincidence, one that shall rightly show what sense your
life has made and makes. Reading this book may be a meaningful
coincidence, one that reveals some new topography of your personal path. Meaningful means destiny-fulfilling. Something about
that destiny is deliberate: we can take a hand in it. This book is
a tool for that work. Synchronicity comes to wake us for a work
we will love, and we will be aroused in time! It is up to us to get
up for the best work we will ever do: a graceful integration of our
psychological and spiritual potential. The "raise" we will get is in
consciousness! This book exhibits the riches of synchronicity and
presents intriguing ways to receive them. The receiving leads to
giving and so every one of us benefits from the work of each of
us. That exchange is the joyous fulfillment of our personal destiny
in a luminous world that longs for light.

Synchronicity is a mind-boggling and sometimes eerie rendezvous between the world and our inner selves. It comforts us with
the mystery of how our human nature and mother nature tell the
same story. In nature, each season produces just the conditions
that the ecology of earth requires. Likewise in our human story,
we keep finding just what we need to evolve as psychological and
spiritual beings. Synchronicity comes as an assisting force in this

11

evolution. Every experience of synchronicity is a daring invitation to let go of ego long enough to design a destiny in accord with the purposes of love.

We are so aware of our limited powers and not quite so aware of our boundless potential. This potential is our true Self, which is unconditionally and universally loving, interiorly wise with the wisdom of the ages, and immensely rich with healing power. When these sleeping powers are activated, we are acting in accord with the best in us. This is the fulfillment of our destiny that fills us with joy. Our spiritual powers may, however, remain a sleeping giant in our psyche and never display themselves in our actions. Then our destiny remains unfulfilled and a sense of something missing may pervade our life. That will not be your fate, reader and worker of this book! By your fidelity to the program of practices in these pages, you will feel yourself deepening in many healthy psychological dimensions and expanding in unguessed spiritual directions. This book is about synchronicity because it is the *signal* that the opportunity has come for this to happen in our lives. Having this book in your hand right now may be how it is happening now.

A series of unusual circumstances or a combination of similar happenings may not be mere coincidence. Synchronicity precipitates events that can suddenly or slowly redirect the course of our life. Such events can be the fulcrum of psychological change and spiritual awakening. Shakespeare wrote: "The very minute bids thee ope' thine ear!" (*The Tempest*). Synchronous moments present just such a bid to us to pay attention to what comes now or next on our journey. Then awkward jolts can become graceful transitions, and stops can become steps. We face our destiny deliberately rather than fall under the spell of fate.

Actually, everything that happens is synchronicity because everything fits perfectly into our life story and its step-by-step advance to destiny. In synchronicity, inside and outside are revealed as appearances. Synchronicity erases the line between us and nature. It blurs the line between the human and the divine.

It underlines the entry of eternity into time. It grants us moments that reveal eternity to be the ground of our being. When we trust this, we take steps from and on that ground. They are dance steps, not a formal ballet but a mirthful jig, at times indecorous or even irreverent. "At the stillpoint, there is the dance," says T. S. Eliot — and there is our destiny.

In this book, we learn how to recognize synchronicity in our daily experience, in our imaginations, and in our dreams. Such heightened awareness leads to a felt sense about what may be incubating in the hidden depths of our unconscious. We then recognize the crucial significance of timing all through our lives and we begin to honor it. Jungian active imagination techniques, Tibetan Buddhist practices, and many other techniques will be combined and applied in the course of these pages so you can work with the phenomenon of synchronicity and gain from it.

This book shows you how to receive the gift of synchronicity so you can open it and discover:

- How to interpret a series of similar happenings

- When to hold on and when to let go

- When to engage and when to make a graceful exit

- How to tell whether people are really for you or against you

- How to open yourself to the assisting forces around you

- How to recognize afflicting forces and gain strength in the face of them

- How to get past the fears that can stop you from being you

- How to understand dreams that correspond to life events

- How to open your potential and be all you really are

- How to deal with fate and participate in your own destiny

- How to face and handle the conditions of existence

- How to tell the right time from the wrong time

- How to use creative imagination in your choices

- How to honor and learn from your dreams

- How to integrate your psychological and spiritual work

- How to live in accord with your deepest needs and wishes

- How to let go of ego and live lovingly

Practical exercises help you access all of the above so that your life can open and expand in new ways. You may never have dreamed it was possible for you to see a miracle. This is a manual on wholeness that hopefully shows you how to see the miracles everywhere around and within you. It presents an intelligent and simple program that gives you a deep sense of personal efficacy and of spiritual connectedness. This book has a side effect: you will notice yourself becoming a person of more depth. In other words, you will really feel and see the underlying significance of your story and the world's story, one and the same.

Spirituality is the intersection of three paths: letting go of ego, an unconditional yes to the conditions of human existence, and an immeasurable compassion. Synchronicity meets us on all three of these paths. These paths open by work on ourselves — steps we take — and by grace from assisting forces around us — shifts and balances that happen. There is synchronicity built into the spiritual model of effort and grace working together! Effortful steps open us to the unexpected miracle of effortless shifts. We work on change, and transformation may happen within that momentum.

Work on ourselves means traveling the three paths of spirituality in psychologically healthy human living. Here is an overview of this work:

- Letting go of ego means freeing ourselves from self-centered entitlements and from the need to be in control. Such letting go is a challenge to the part of us that insists on being first and right. It is a non-violent style that drops competitiveness and self-seeking in favor of humility and equality. Synchronously, just the right people and events will come our way so that this can happen. We will definitely get our comeuppance and be liberated from our ego inflations as we meet up with our fellow pilgrims!

• We say yes unconditionally to the conditions and predicaments of our existence: things change and end, suffering is part of growth, things are not always predictable or fair, etc. We assent to these givens of life because we trust them as necessary ingredients for us to grow and deepen. Spiritual progress does not mean that I am always serene or happy but that I have a formula to accommodate any state of mind: an unconditional yes to what is unfolding. This yes is how we *become* synchronicity. We identify our personal story with a larger picture. We ride in the same direction the horse is going.

• Compassion means acting in such a way that all beings are happy, at peace, and fulfilled by enlightenment. A personal awakening brings with it an inner zeal for others to be awakened too. This emerges from a sense of solidarity with all beings and with all of nature — the very point of synchronicity! The result is no distinction between time and timelessness, subject and object, male and female, humankind and nature. Such a transcendence of apparent opposites is spiritual synchronicity at work. When Thomas Merton wrote books of comfort about meditation, he was widely read and well received by the public. When he spoke out against Vietnam and in favor of pacifism as the tangible practice of meditation, he was shunned by the majority of his former readers. *Tikkun ʿolam* is a phrase in the Hebrew Kabbalah meaning: repair of the world. Such engaged concern is the proof positive of an authentic spirituality which does not end in "feel good" but in "do good." It is not about consolation for our minds but consecration of our hearts to this needy world.

All three paths of spirituality lead to freedom from our habitual attachment to fear and acquisitiveness. The final challenge of spirituality is always the giving of ourselves. In fact, giving is the best way to free ourselves from the fears and attachments that make us so unhappy! Spirituality is another means to the only end that can be worthy of beings like us: love. *Can I dedicate myself now*

*to finding more and more love within myself and then to turning
everything I learn in this book into good deeds?*

St. Thomas Aquinas says that a miracle is unusual, like a healing, not routine like a sunrise. It has to be unexpected, a surprise,
the result of a power beyond human making. It is an amazing
grace! Synchronicities are unusual, unexpected, not constructed
by the human ego. In this sense they are miracles of conjunction
between ourselves and the events of the world. When we reconcile
ourselves to the conditions of our existence, when we reconcile
the opposing forces in our psyche, when we reconcile ourselves to
those who have hurt us, many stunning marvels begin to happen.
We cannot cause miracles, but we can greet them and grant them
hospitality in the yet unopened rooms of our souls. Then the unexpected, unsuspected miracles are respected! These pages show
how that can happen.

The human organism comes equipped with self-healing powers.
We have three reliable and highly skilled healers, three graces,
within ourselves. The first is an inner physician — the grace of
the body — who rushes to the scene of an accident. We cut a finger and he brings platelets to stop the bleeding and white cells to
prevent infection. We can cooperate in this process by washing
and covering the cut, skills we learned from our first aid manual.

We also embody an inner psychologist — the grace of the
psyche — who knows just how to help us with our emotional injuries. When a shocking loss occurs, she brings tears of mourning
to the site of the wound. We join in by griefwork, which includes
allowing our feelings to emerge, taking time off from work, and
even being depressed for a while. We can trust our inner psychologist to have a handy program perfectly calibrated for every crisis
that may come along. To make that program more effective and
expeditious we have to work along with it.

Finally, we are aware of the metaphor of the guardian angel.
This is our inner priest, our spiritual guide — the grace of the
soul — who knows the full itinerary of our journey through life
and can offer the provisions it requires. The sacraments he ad-

ministers are the ones that are meaningful from our religious heritage. In addition, he brings these: synchronicity, dreams, intuitions, bursts of imagination, spontaneous creativity, sudden awakenings, and other miracles. We participate by faithful attention, and then by acting in accord with the callings of our destiny. The skills for this work are presented in this book.

The physical work leads to the joy of health. The psychological work leads to the joy of responsible living and effective relating. The spiritual work leads to the joy of universal love. Our work in all three areas is to synchronize our learned skills with our inborn resources. This is the dance, the harmonized movements of effort and grace that enact the equation of human wholeness. Personal power is an abiding and inviolable trust that the three graces are resident and active in our psyches. It is synchronicity at work — or rather, at play!

My personal purpose in life as psychotherapist, teacher, and writer is to point to this source in all of us. My books, and most specifically this one, are meant as manuals to assist our inner psychologist and our inner priest in their luminous work. I am hoping to build our confidence in the trustworthy light inside us and to cultivate the skills to let it come through. I especially hope this happens to the person holding this book in his/her hands right now.

This book is not new-age but age-old in its perspectives. It combines a theoretical understanding with specific practices. By working on the suggestions in the text and in the practice sections, you will know, more deeply than ever, what your life has been about and where it can go. Knowledge without love is as inadequate as love without expression. The meaningful activation of concepts matters more than an intellectual grasp of them. The practices are carefully constructed and built upon one another to help you make your personal journey through and for our evolving universe: we need the world for our unfolding and the world needs us for its unfolding. Good psychology is ecology.

Synchronicity is explicitly pointed out in the text about half the time. Yet it appears on every page! You will notice synchronicity in the many references that show coincidence, similitude, resemblance, and metaphor. The main concepts of the book are revisited throughout the text, each time in the context of a higher level of consciousness. "I" statements appear throughout these pages. It may be helpful to highlight them and copy them into your journal. They can become affirmations for you, wherever appropriate.

You are about to be accompanied through a sequence of learnings and experiences that will facilitate change in your life. This is an accompaniment in the sense of musical accompaniment to the music in your soul and the music of the spheres — which are, of course, one and the same. This is the essence of the speech from *The Merchant of Venice* in the epigraph at the beginning of this book. It will be referred to often throughout the text. It is an exquisitely complete and touching articulation of all this book attempts, so haltingly, to say. Look at it now before reading the paragraph that follows.

What a precious and privileged destiny we humans have: to become the escorts who ease the entrance of light and love into the world. We are honor guards in a long procession of forbears and followers, who, like us, are always en route and always already here among the stars.

> *We spend our lives waiting for the great day, the great battle, or the great deed of power. But that external consummation is not given to many, nor is it necessary. So long as our being is tensed passionately into the spirit in everything, then that spirit will emerge from our own hidden, nameless efforts. . . . Right from the hands that knead the dough to the hands that consecrate it, only one Host is being made.*
>
> —Pierre Teilhard de Chardin

Chapter One

SYNCHRONICITY: How Moment Becomes Momentum

What Is Synchronicity?

Synchronicity is the phenomenon of meaningful coincidence. It is a resemblance, concurrence, correspondence, or connection between something going on outside us and something happening inside us. In any ordinary coincidence, the events are connected by meaning rather than by cause and effect. This may not yet be synchronicity but simply synchronization. It becomes synchronicity when it makes a meaningful connection with our life's purposes or helps unfold our destiny to show love, see wisely, and bring healing to ourselves and our world. All coincidences are connected by meaning, but synchronicity happens when the meaningfulness is relevant to our personal evolution. It is the spur of the moment in that it spurs us on and in that it may happen suddenly! It happens just in time. It is also *just* in time in the sense that it is part of the justice of the universe in bringing us exactly the pieces we need to fashion — or be fashioned by — our destiny.

Synchronicity is a word made from two Greek terms meaning "joined with" and "time." Synchronicity is a bond or connection that happens in a timely way. A correspondence between two things is suddenly made clear. The unifying connection was always present but an immediate and meaningful coincidence makes it visible here and now. Synchronicity thus combines an essential unity with an existential one. The eternal present makes an appearance in the momentary present. This is why it seems fitting to say that synchronicity guides us into spirituality.

Here is a simple example of the difference between synchronicity and synchronization: I am afraid to dive, and while at the pool, I see someone teaching his son to dive so I watch and learn. This was a simple coincidence, synchronization of need and resource. Because of my learning to dive, my confidence builds and I eventually become a diving teacher, start a diving school, and even help an Olympic hopeful! I can trace it all back to my first eavesdropping and experimenting at the pool. This makes that original event synchronicity. Later, I unexpectedly find myself reading this book and its chapter on crisis brings me to a new depth of understanding! I find that in ancient times, diving from a high cliff was an initiatory sacrament, representing a plunge into the unknown waters of rebirth: a primitive form of baptism. This enriches my own experience of my spiritual work. Now the synchronicity has reached me more deeply and the grace of it has appeared more clearly. I have entered the realm of the miraculous.

Synchronicities cluster around significant events. Many meaningful coincidences occurred, for instance, when the *Titanic* sank and when Lincoln and Kennedy were assassinated. Personal disasters or crises in our personal life will also invite synchronicity. Norma orders a red dress for a party but a black dress is delivered to her. As she is about to phone the store to report the error, her sister calls: "Mother has died. Come for the funeral." Norma thought she was in control of her life; she thought she knew what would happen next. The synchronous event told her otherwise and outfitted her for what was actually coming next: something much deeper was about to occur.

Synchronicity is the surprise that something suddenly fits! Synchronous events are meaningful coincidences or correspondences that guide us, warn us, or confirm us on our path. Coincidence happens at a specific moment. In this sense it is existential, tied to the here and now. Correspondences are ongoing. This is how synchronicity is essential, always present, to our human experience. Synchronicity is also found in a series of similar events or experiences. It can appear as one striking event that sets off a chain reaction. It is always unexpected and somehow uncanny in its accuracy of connection or revelation. This is what makes it impossible to dismiss synchronicity as mere coincidence.

Jung called synchronicity "a non-causal but meaningful relationship between physical and psychic events,... a special instance of acausal orderedness.... Conscious succession becomes simultaneity.... Synchronicity takes the events in space and time as meaning more than mere chance." A coincidence is two unplanned events that happen simultaneously. It becomes synchronicity when it is connected by meaning. You and I love red roses. That is a coincidence. If unknown to each other, we meet as our heads bump while we are both smelling the same red rose that caught our eye at the same time and then later, we are married, that is synchronicity!

Synchronicity is the counterpart to cause/effect connections. In synchronicity, the link is forged by meaningfulness, not by linear reaction of cause to effect. Since the Self is not bound by linear time, it is possible to have another model for succession. Instead of one thing following another, there can also be instances in which things happen together. Simultaneity takes the place of linear progression in the timeless world of the psyche. Synchronicity is the word for this alternative.

Synchronicity represents a perfect paradox. A paradox is an apparent contradiction that is nonetheless true. There is an apparent contradiction between multiplicity and unity. Yet, in synchronicity, two events become one in significance. The existential display of two circumstances, one of which may be external and one internal, are essentially one in meaningfulness. An analogy might be in ancient herbalism. The law of signatures referred to the similarity between certain plants and parts of the human body. It was believed that this resemblance meant that the herb had healing qualities for that organ. In homeopathy, the law of similars is also an example: one is healed by what ails one. In both instances, similitude and symmetry are vehicles to wholeness.

The Self is a field of perpetual possibility in time and of infinite possibility in space. Its potential is in the vast extent of its love, wisdom, and healing power, in people and in all of nature. For these potentials to be actualized in us requires the creative commitment of the ego to love generously, to access intuitive wisdom, and to bring balance to the world and to human relationships. Synchronicity is a message from the Self to the ego about how to trust this and about how to do it.

Synchronicity gives us a clue to the deep underlay of purpose and meaning in the universe and how that purpose is working itself out in our lives. Our own wholeness has a foundation and support in the larger order of things. All objective events have a corresponding subjective configuration in our psyche. Synchronicity is an instant instance of this correspondence. Its spontaneous timely events are articulations of the continuous nature of creation, intimations about the irrefrangible unity underlying it. Synchronicity is always striking and sometimes eerie. The "otherworldly" feeling we have when it happens to us may be an indicator that an archetype is arising into consciousness from the depths of our psyche.

Synchronicity is an unexpected significant coincidence between an external event and an internal readiness for a change or a transition. Some events are coincidences in that they touch off a chain reaction on our journey, e.g., a painful loss leads eventually to a surprisingly positive outcome. Sometimes an unusual event sets in motion a series of changes or a whole new direction in our life. In such synchronicity the event can be critical or minor, a loss or a gain, a correct choice or an error, something voluntary or involuntary. "We do not know whether the things afflicting us are the secret beginning of our happiness or not," wrote Jorge Luis Borges.

Things happen as they need to for the best purposes of the universe. Our belief that we can interfere with this is another trick of the arrogant ego. We may not know how what is happening right now really fits into our future. I can only trust that in addition to all I see, there is some other vision that will appear and make all this appear as just right.

Synchronicity may appear in this specific symptom I now face, in this depression I am in, in this quandary that obsesses me. I may find in any of these painful experiences a new potential for self-healing or a new direction on my journey. There is a healing predisposition in the psyche to produce just the spurs we need and just in time.

Synchronicity also works by presenting an unconscious image (as yet unknown to us) which comes to us directly or symbolically as a dream, intuition, or premonition. This may correspond to an existing life situation with an identical meaning. To perceive this meaning requires a coincidence of two psychic events: a normal knowledge of the causal world and an interruption of the normal state by an archetypal constellation. When these two are simultaneous, the experience is synchronous.

Consecutive events in life make up the exterior order of our existence. An interior order manifests itself in dreams and synchronicity, which show us the hidden acausal order of things. Sudden intuitions or moments of truth are synchronous because they represent explicating moments in which the greater cosmic meaning of our life becomes visible. The function of intuition is to reveal the vast field of possibility in this one moment of insight. Intuition is thus a springboard to the release of our inner immense potential. This is why intuition is a spiritual gift that opens the Self to its destiny.

Synchronicity shows us the latent meaning of our human archetypes — inner dispositions to live out challenges to our versatility. Ordinary coincidences are not synchronicity. They become synchronicity only when they are or prove to be meaningful, that is, related to our journey/destiny toward/of wholeness. To be synchronicity, the meaningfulness of the coincidence also has to be evident to us. When there is no observer of a meaning-

ful coincidence, it is not synchronicity but simply "synchronization."

Yet synchronicity cannot happen by any conscious intervention of ego since it is a phenomenon of grace: an entry of the
transpersonal world onto our personal turf. It is a moment that
manifests the unity that always and already existed between psychological and spiritual, mind and universe, you and me, me
and everything. It occurs when our unconscious is ready for a
step into wider consciousness. The ancient oracles were about
precisely this!

The inner artist of our true Self uses two brushes: a conscious
one, synchronicity, and an unconscious one, dreams. The synchronicities (meaningful coincidences) of our lives and the dream
images that have most excited or stupefied us are the best —
though often most ambiguous — clues to our self-actualization.
When a dream confirms a movement in the psyche, that is itself synchronicity. Prayer that is answered is synchronicity, since
prayers that are answered are the ones that are consistent with
our destiny.

Synchronicity is actually calibrated into the psyche in two
ways. Since opposites constellate and combine there, if we become
too one-sided consciously, our psyche will shower us with synchronous events, dreams, and relationships that commandeer us
gently to the other side. For instance, if we are overly controlling,
things will happen that topple our house of cards. To work with
synchronicity is to go along with such a program and lighten up
on ourselves and others.

Sometimes, however, the ego is meant only to maintain or contain a tension of opposites without making a choice in favor of
either. This prompts the psyche to release a healing third dimension. This "transcendent function" is the synchronous capacity to
present us with exactly the reconciling or balancing image that
unites or cuts through our either...or's. This miracle of paradox
allows a whole new possibility to open for us. It happens to us
when we simply do not take sides with either opponent in the

inner argument. For example, I am alone now that you are gone. I have grieved your loss. Now I can start looking for someone new or I can continue to avoid connecting with anyone else. I decide not to seek but certainly not to avoid. And, spontaneously, along comes someone who is neither pushy nor passive. Or, along comes an opportunity for a whole new focus in my career and I find such great sources of nurturance in it that relationship becomes less important for now. Maybe later that very career turn will introduce me to someone new.

Thus, our psyche is the algebra expert with two favorite ways of reaching a pleasing equation: it can compensate for onesidedness by dealing the opposite to us. Or it can factor out a third solution to us as we are holding two alternatives and not acting on either. The unique shapes of the synchronicities that cluster around us tell us which program is in place.

Synchronicity is the special moment in which destiny summons us to move forward. It is, as we saw above, the spur of the moment that initiates movement and may at the same time smart! This is the process by which archetypal reality incarnates itself in historical time: something unknown is doing we do not know what or why or through whom. Synchronicity really means that we are never alone in the universe. "O mighty love! Man is one world, and hath another to attend him," wrote George Herbert.

Many psychic events do not occur instantaneously but undergo an incubation period in the unconscious. Something has not yet happened but is in the works. Synchronicity cuts across timebound warps. It transcends the limits of being and becoming. This is because in the inner world there is no separation between past and future, time or timelessness, what is happening, what is about to happen, and what will happen. Only the present exists, which contains it all. In synchronicity, we meet our future — or our past — in our present. "To transform itself in us the future enters into us long before it happens," Rainer Maria Rilke wrote.

Synchronicity sometimes pieces itself together over days or months or even years: I was climbing in the mountains of Crete this year when I suddenly realized that they had a voice. The next month I was climbing to the top of Mount Sinai and I remembered that Moses heard a voice that drew him up this same mountain. That was the voice I must have meant in Crete, I thought. That evening, I was sitting with Father Paul, one of the monks of St. Catherine's monastery at the foot of Mount Sinai. He said: "The mountains pray." The voice was now speaking to me, asking me to hear it or even to find my voice in its own.

Finally, is synchronicity a form of superstition? Superstition is an irrational belief in a cause/effect connection when there is none in reality, e.g., a black cat crossing my path produces bad luck. Synchronicity is an alternative to cause/effect. It is acausal. The connection is based on a rational meaning, not irrational belief. Superstition is maintained by ignorance of the laws of nature or by false faith in magic or chance. Synchronicity is supported by a long-standing wisdom about the correlation between a coincidence and something spiritual that is afoot. It respects and is mediated through nature, and it abrogates the belief in chance altogether.

To appreciate synchronicity as it is treated in this book requires a conviction that meanings are discovered, not imputed. The bias in these chapters is that an objective value exists irrespective of whether it is acknowledged as such by a subjective observer. In fact, synchronicity is founded on a trust that there *is* meaning in the world but that this meaning *appears* only when we are open to it. A piano sonata of Mozart strikes Jeckel with deep, unnamable, life-affecting meaning. Heckel scoffs at it as cacophony and receives nothing from it at all. The essential (abiding) value is in the sonata. Its existential (here and now) meaningfulness is in the hearer. This is why the full phenomenon of synchronicity requires that someone become conscious of it as a meaningful coincidence. Even the most spiritual events wait for our human yes. This is the loving respect of the divine for the human.

Synchronicity at a Glance

What to look for in synchronicity:

- Coincidence, correspondence, connection, resemblance

- Trigger-points to a series of events or turning points

- The unexpected, unusual, uncanny, improbable

- What happens on the spur of the moment and just in time

- What is meaningful, is revelatory, and has become conscious to us

- The fluke or choice or happenstance that uncovers a whole new possibility in our psyche or a most useful path to our true bliss

- Serendipity, finding good fortune by accident, which is a way of referring to the playful dimension of synchronicity

Since synchronicity is an advantageous juxtaposition or turning point that occurs spontaneously and unexpectedly in the course of life, it happens beyond our control, i.e., by a grace. This makes it feel uncanny or strange but yet welcome and confirming. It is meaningful in that it increases our consciousness, i.e., casts the light of consciousness onto something that was hidden. Something is meaningful when it reveals or exposes the bond between the ego and the Self, uniting apparent opposites so that wholeness can come into full view.

Synchronicity invites or challenges us to become more capable of loving, and/or of accessing wisdom, and/or of becoming a source of healing and peace. The actualization of these potentials *is* our destiny. We do not create our destiny; we participate in its unfolding. Synchronicity happens as an activating assistance toward the design of that destiny. It can help us in this way because it is a numinous visit of the transcendent/transpersonal into our transitory/personal world. Synchronicity is thus a major tool of soul-making, divulging immortal meanings through personal events so that we can find our way toward integration.

PRACTICE

The suggestions that follow, like all those in this book, are meant to help you work *with* synchronicity in two ways. You learn to recognize synchronicities and follow them up with practices that take their cues, always uniquely designed by your higher Self to move you toward your destiny of wholeness.

• Keep track of any coincidences that happen as you read this book. Notice which of them become meaningful, i.e., bring out the best in you, change your perspective in such a way that new things can happen to you, make you more loving, or wiser, or more able to help or heal yourself or others. Now you are in the realm of synchronicity. Parse a personal message from these experiences, one that moves you along on your journey. This happens when you challenge yourself to act in new ways, to go out of character, to be more authentic about your deepest needs and wishes, and to have a sense of mission: "I am here to share the gifts I was given." The habit of giving in response to what you are receiving is the way to work spiritually with synchronicity. It is the balance of opposites that advances a spiritual momentum already begun in synchronicity. If you do not have a spiritual director, share your experiences with the friend who seems most spiritually conscious and listen to his or her feedback. Take the feedback as an extension of the synchronicity that touched off this process of finding your own mission. What purpose of the universe wants to work itself out in you? How has it already begun? How have you participated in it or sabotaged it?

• Look at the significant events in your life and explore the synchronicities that happen around them. What message was trying to come through? Look at events that seemed negative at first and then turned into something good. What synchronicities clustered around those events? Now look at your present life. If synchronicity happens around an event that seems negative to you now, there may be something positive in the works. Find a good in the bad and look for ways to expand on it.

• Pay attention to the surprises that happen to you. What do they call you to uncover? Are you setting up your life so that there will be no surprises? Is everything too orderly? What do you lose that way? Is fear behind your not being surprised very much these days?

• What are some correspondences, similarities, or serendipities that have happened this month? How do they warn, guide, or confirm you? What may be afoot in your life? What new freedom in you may be endeavoring to be born by lightening you of what you have been carrying for so long. Perhaps there are obligations that you want to be done with. Or perhaps there are things you may be loath to lose, but the time has come for them to go.

• What are the images — or one image — that come up over and over for you? How do they point to something you are ready to go for or to let go of? Is there a need or want in you that is not being fulfilled? Does not the synchronicity of an image that continually fascinates you call you to follow it through?

• Consider the problem or symptom that nags at you physically or emotionally. It may be a synchronous repetition that symbolizes a deep cry or yearning that you have failed to acknowledge. Give it a hearing and follow what it says. Do this by dialoguing with the symptom or problem in written form. Look particularly for the gift dimension of the symptom that plagues you. Since we contain all the opposites, there is a valuable kernel in even the most hard-shell suffering. It might be in a lesson that you learn. It might be in the opening of a new room in your psyche, a new space for a deeper version of yourself. It might be in the engendering of compassion for others who suffer as you do.

• Are you noticing yourself to be too one-sided in your attitudes or modus operandi? Are you faced with a dilemma in which

there are two opposite possibilities tugging at you and you do not
want to choose either? Notice any coincidences that have happened around these issues. Look at your dream images too. What
do the images and synchronicities say to you about your present
predicament? Are you being moved to act out an opposite style of
your usual way of being and behaving? Are you being prompted
to sit with both sides of an issue and not feel forced to act in favor
of either? Picture yourself in each of these circumstances. Which
one feels just right?

Autumn brings typhoons in Japan, so the farmer is faced with
a dilemma: work hard at pulling weeds or let them grow, since
there may not even be a harvest:

> *I do no know if autumn will bring rain or storm,*
> *And I shall pull the weeds in the rice paddies.*

Asynchrony: When the Time Is All Wrong

Asynchrony is the opposite of synchronicity. We become aware,
through a series of negating coincidences, that this is the wrong
time for ventures. Nothing works; doors keep closing. We find
ourselves involved in wars of attrition, obeying laws of diminish-
ing returns.

At the end of *King Lear*, the Duke of Albany offers to share
his authority with Kent and Edgar, both of whom refuse. *Kent:* "I
have a journey, sir, shortly to go / My master calls me; I must not
say no." *Edgar:* "The weight of this sad time we must obey." Both
characters read their own times accurately. Reading the hand-
writing on the wall is often a way of describing asynchrony, an
indication that this is not the time for success but rather that our
time is almost up in this area and we are ready for new options
elsewhere. We can yank the figs from the tree in early summer
and find only a hard, unpalatable taste, unsatisfying and flat. In

late summer, they will yield with ease to the slightest tug; they are synchronously sweet.

Asynchrony is a challenge to the "little engine that could" or the "any man can be president" ego-inflating (or ultimately ego-deflating) mentality that we inherited from public school. The danger is in the absolutizing of the message in such a way that trying hard becomes the only acceptable plan. It is sometimes true that effort is expedient. However, it is also sometimes true that letting go for now or for good is necessary. For those in tune with the universe and its soulful powers, messages will come to us in synchronicity, in dreams, and in inner images that reveal which is the appropriate path. It will not be based on maxims but on the maximum series of messages that point to a particular path.

Asynchrony appears in relationships in a variety of ways. It is in the mismatching and incompatibility of some partners. It shows itself in reverse displays of intimacy and distance between partners: I draw near when you pull back and vice versa. We may keep doing what does not work no matter how we try to change the pattern. Asynchrony can appear in a relationship when one partner fears abandonment so much that he continually clings and doubts his partner's fidelity. The partner feels engulfed and creates distance. Then the one who feared abandonment is unfaithful and it is she who does the abandoning!

Paying attention is the first requisite for finding asynchrony. The second is letting go of the inflated ego belief that "it has to be my way," or the belief that "it has to be one way." Sometimes, synchronicity and asynchrony combine in differing directions. At the end of *Romeo and Juliet* we discover that what is asynchrony for the young couple is synchronicity for their families. Death for Romeo and Juliet leads to reconciliation for the rest of the family.

> *I cannot force a butterfly to emerge before its time,*
> *I cannot pull the budded petals of the rose away to make it*
>   *look at if it were in bloom.*

PRACTICE

What are you trying hard to achieve in your life at the moment? Do you notice that nothing works to make it happen? Putting in all the effort you can is a good rule of thumb. But when do you draw the line and say: "That's it. It's time to let go and move on." There is no infallible way to know if you would do better to keep at it or to give up and move on. The following criteria of asynchrony may be helpful. *Let it go if your efforts:*

- are depleting you

- are being experienced as intrusive by others

- feel forced — like kicking against the goad

- yield less and less

- prevent you from trying a whole new option that awaits you elsewhere

- seem anachronistic — no longer in character for you at this age or at this level of consciousness

- are based on childhood messages of how you are supposed to succeed or be the strong one, no matter what

- contradict the clear message of someone who is saying no in every way she can as you keep trying for a yes

- are based on wishful thinking rather than what the record shows

Apply the above criteria to something you are trying hard to accomplish: What are you trying to get your children, partner, friends, parents, etc. to be or become? What are you trying to make yourself into? What are you pushing with no result? Is this stubbornness or intelligent effort? Ask for feedback from someone you trust.

Our Psyche: The Soulscape of Synchronicity

It is easier to sail many thousands of miles through cold and storm...than to explore the private sea, the Atlantic and Pacific of one's being alone.   —Henry David Thoreau (*Walden*)

Our ego is the center of our conscious rational life. It has our name and body. It is functional and healthy when it helps us fulfill our goals in life: happiness within ourselves, effectiveness in our tasks, and fulfilling relationships. The ego becomes dysfunctional and neurotic when it distracts us from our goals or sabotages them. Behind every neurosis is a fear that has never been addressed or resolved. "Neurotic" means being caught in useless repetition of archaic ways of protecting ourselves against what no longer truly threatens us. This is why Jung defines neurosis as "a defeat by the unreal." We know we are integrating ourselves effectively and are on a valid spiritual path when we simultaneously remain functional and balanced in daily life.

The Self is a spiritual source rather than a psychological resource. Jung called the Self "the God archetype" within. It includes the ego and is the center and circumference of the entire psyche. It is a field of inner gravity that is sometimes unconscious and sometimes conscious. Jung theorized that our unconscious is both personal, containing the family album of our own memories, and cosmic, containing the mythic memories of humankind. This collective unconscious, he said, "contains the whole spiritual heritage of mankind's evolution, born anew in the brain structure of every individual."

Our ego is in us; we are in the Self. Ego is the bearer of our personality. The Self is unlimited by individual personality. It has no name. It is the same threefold reality in everyone: unconditional love, eternal wisdom, and the power to heal ourselves and others. It is mediated into the world by its incarnation: our body/ego. We might say that *the ego is our capacity for light and the Self is the light.*

Our human enterprise is to form or find an equilibrium, an axis, between ego and Self. We thereby unleash the powers of the Self from the stranglehold of our frightened, limiting ego and let them flow into the world. We were born with more potential than actuality. Our task is to activate our potentials, to make them conscious, i.e., articulated in our lifetime. This is how we let the light of consciousness through. Astronomer Tim Ferris says: "Consciousness is like a campfire in the middle of a dark Australia." Spirituality is igniting ourselves so that such a wonderful thing can happen.

Our psychological work is to shape our ego so that it can function well. This brings all our talents into the service of the Self and drafts our every thought, word, and deed into showing all the love we can in one lifetime. The neurotic ego contravenes this work by its prejudice that we are separate, in control, and licensed to have all our needs met. The *Course in Miracles* says: "Your choice to use this device [ego] *enables* it to endure." Our psychological work is to dismantle our neurotic ego in favor of our functional ego.

Our ego is functional when it is leading us to our goals in life: to live happily, to be productive in our choice of work, and to have satisfying and effective relationships. If I want to go north, my body is functional when I walk in a northerly direction. If I walk south to go north, something has become dysfunctional, i.e., neurotic. The functional ego is the best vehicle for the emergence of the Self.

St. John of the Cross wrote: "Swiftly, with nothing spared, I am being completely dismantled." This is the true fate of the neurotic ego. Nothing less is required for spiritual growth than the total dissolution of the inflated ego. Inflation is the habit of imagining and acting as if the whole purpose of life was one's own aggrandizement. Aggrandizement means bringing attention only to our own needs, demanding to be in control, believing we are entitled to be served by everyone and to have the ordinary conditions of existence repealed or relaxed for us. Intimate relationships provide the most powerful provocations for the dismantling of the illusions of our controlling and entitled egos!

The neurotic side of the ego is not meant to be destroyed but, paradoxically, to be expanded so that it can extend its creative possibilities to all our psyche. It is liberated by being relieved of its arrogance and then opened to its potential for power *for* rather than power *over* others. This is also our potential for bringing peace into the world and into our relationships. A hero is a person who lives through the pain of this process and is thereby transformed by it. This transformation reveals us to ourselves as singular and as one with all that is: "All the lotus lands and all the Buddhas are revealed in my own being," says the Avatamsaka Sutra. The Self is the Buddha nature.

Our psyche is driven by a spontaneous urge toward wholeness and strives to harmonize polarities: conscious and unconscious, ego and Self. It is up to us to animate this process with tangible actions or to let it slumber. Our lively affirmations might be: "I feel a homing instinct for wholeness. I do what it takes to break the spell of ego." Joseph Campbell says: "Hell is being stuck in ego." He is referring to the neurotic ego with its compulsive attachment to fear and desire. The first noble truth in Buddhism is that all is suffering. Such suffering in our lives is the best clue we have that we may be clinging (desire) or running (fear). So the first noble truth of Buddhism ("All is suffering") is actually: all is ego!

Contemplate this image: St. Paul is sitting, arrogant and erect, on his high horse of ego. Now see him under the horse's hoofs: lower than an animal. That is how it feels to be divested of ego; it is that dramatic! Humility is hell for the ego! If hell is being stuck in ego, then becoming unstuck must be as difficult as getting out of the worst hell!

Our functional ego adapts to the external world by socialized behavior and extroversion (mediated by our persona: the appearance we make to others). It adapts to the internal world by introversion (mediated by our shadow: the dark side of us that we hide from others and from ourselves). Our ego becomes more and more functional by disidentifying with any exclusive attachment to our persona, by reclaiming shadow projections, and by recovering our body as a legitimate and useful tool in the adventure of living. The shadow is the part of us that is hidden and unconscious to us. Our negative shadow contains all that we strongly detest in ourselves but cannot see. We tend to see this shadow of ours in others: detesting in them exactly what is disowned in us. Our positive shadow holds our untapped potential. We admire in others what is buried and deactivated in us!

HEALTHY EGO:

Resources:

Observe

Assess

Act in accord with goals

Make choices that reflect our deepest wishes, values, powers, and needs

SPIRITUAL SELF:

The Source:

Unconditional love, perennial wisdom, and healing power

The work is to return to the source through the healthy ego's resources. The source is within. It is the Self beyond the clinging ego: my Buddha nature perfect in essence but imperfectly exhibited in my daily existence. So there is a perfect bee but not a perfect me: I have to work at being who and all that I already am.

The Inflated Ego at a Glance

Spiritual awakening involves maintaining a healthy ego and letting go of the inflated — neurotic — ego with its central theme of retaliation:

- becomes enraged, spiteful, and vindictive when thwarted, found to be in error, or bested (even in games or sports)

- has to win: cannot be second, will not be last

- has to be right, noticed, and praised

- holds a grudge and has to get even

- will not forgive or forget

- has to have its own way: controlling, demanding, manipulative

- is abusive, sarcastic, territorial, possessive

- shows hierarchical (not cooperative) dominance, has to be in charge

- has to be appreciated for every good deed

- has to be excused for every misdeed: denies misbehavior or need for amends

- cannot be criticized or even given negative feedback

- demands an exemption from the conditions of existence

- demands love, respect, and loyalty no matter what

- cannot lose face (lose ego) or apologize

- cannot be taught anything, acknowledge fault, or be wrong

- has to come out looking good

- is concerned with how things will look, appearances

- has to return a favor (keep it even, don't be beholden to anyone)

- cannot need others or be dependent on them in any way

- finds flexibility or compromise impossible

- overreacts to minor slights, would rather die than sustain a major insult

Note the compulsive, aggressive — and painful — flavor of all the above.

The inflated ego is compulsive since it *has* to act in these ways, lest it lose control or the rank it believes itself entitled to at any cost to its own peace of mind. In fact there is no peace when ego rules. It is aggressive because of the "me first" attitude and the retaliatory, punitive flavor of so much of the ego style. It is painful because those who act from a neurotic ego are full of fear, feel terribly anxious about losing face, and notice that, though they may win, they certainly are not successful at being loved. In a job in which they have even minimal authority, they may demand rigid adherence to the rules, lord it over others, and strongly punish those who defy their authority.

Sometimes ego can be confused with self-reliance. The following may reflect self-reliance *or* ego:

- "I won't give up (or in)."

- "I keep my word."

- "I said I'll do it and I will."

An example of the capacity of the ego to sustain its rage and indignation is in the instance of the divorced man who kidnaps his children and keeps them away from their mother for years. Another might be someone who refuses to talk to a friend for years after a single instance of being snubbed. One affront, even unintended, can keep the ego angry and mean-spirited for the rest of one's life!

The essence of the neurotic ego is the terror of having to face the conditions of existence without control over them or entitlement to exemption from them. In healthy relating my ego-control is deposed in favor of equality. Entitlement becomes asking for what I want with the understanding that I may not get it! My indignation (ego anger) then shows itself as sadness about not being loved as I wanted to be and, paradoxically, I become much more lovable!

 # PRACTICE

Here are some declarations that help to reverse the ego's devices:

- I give up having to get my way.
- I let go of controlling and manipulating others.
- I ask for appreciation, understanding, and love and let go of demanding them.
- I admit when I am wrong and quickly make amends.
- I invite others to call me on my mistakes.
- I accept the fact that I do not always win or gain or find fairness.
- I make no demands; I ask for what I want and can take no for an answer.
- I am fully responsible for my behavior.
- I love, respect, and give preference to others.
- I forego the wish or plan to punish or get even.
- I forego the desire and plan to retaliate.
- I am becoming truer to my higher Self where unconditional love abounds.
- As I let my ego urges be dissolved, I discover and uncover my indestructible Self.

Note the generous sweetness of all the above.

The work may be scary: to stand on the brink of vengeance and to feel the urgency to do it and the clear sense of righteousness, but not to jump that way. Love's forgiving arms await me in the meadow, where "the lilac with mastering odor holds me" (Walt Whitman).

Show "The Inflated Ego at a Glance" section of this chapter (see above, p. 36) to three people: your significant other or best friend, the person who criticizes you the most, and a member of your family of origin. Ask each of them to suggest which listings seem to apply to you. Thank each of them without putting up any argument. Then write out the above affirmations and work with the ones that you agree apply to you.

Losing/Saving Face

In each of the above declarations, the fear of grieving is transformed into a willingness to grieve. This is a consent to, rather than a dispute with, one of the conditions of existence: losses happen and can be mourned and let go of.

The ego is inflated when its main concern is saving face — F.A.C.E.: Fear, Attachment, Control, and Entitlement. The ego does not know its first name (fear), only its last name (entitlement)! To be caught in the rigidities of the arrogant ego is to live in fear. Transformation is letting love no longer be only a letting in but also a letting through. This can happen because love was behind the fear all the while, waiting for a chance to come through and then to expand through us to everyone else. We provide the Self that chance when we let go of ego. This is what is meant by saying that spirituality (and ultimately compassion) begins with the dismantling of ego. Wisdom-compassion means that you have finally seen through your habit of self-aggrandizement. Once you see how much of your creative energy you sunk into saving F.A.C.E., you see everyone else doing the same useless thing and compassion happens.

It seems that it is healthy not to care too much about others' opinions of you. To say that others' opinions and reactions to you do not matter does not mean that others do not matter. It is only to say that you have an immovable center of great value and that no one can supplant it, or is needed to enhance it. Freedom from fear and craving protects the soul's core with healthy boundaries. A healthy ego sets these boundaries and maintains them. In this sense, there are no significant relationships. No one can be significant enough to change or stop me. That happens only when I relax my boundaries and allow it.

It follows from all this that people and events that challenge and deflate my ego are assisting forces of my soul. Each is a personification of grace. Ego enemies are friends of my Self. The woman who betrayed me, the boss who fired me, the son who turned against me, the friend who called me on my selfishness, the teacher who showed me how much I needed to learn may all have been players in my touching drama of liberation from ego. Each helped me by giving me the opportunity to let go of my arrogant entitlements in favor of humility and vulnerability, the antechambers to the throne-room of real love. The fact that just the right people appeared at just the right time in just the right place is stunning synchronicity.

The afflicting forces in our story were the fear-driven people and institutions that imposed the shoulds and rigid restrictions that were self-limiting, not self-protecting. They were *guards* over our freedom. The assisting forces were those who provided flexibility and liberty to experience and experiment. They were the *guardians* of our freedom. *Who comes to mind?*

Warrior energy applied to the dismantling of ego takes two forms: taking hold and letting go/letting be. The warrior's work is done by self-discipline, ultimately a form of healthy self-love. Self-denial (ego denial!) is "not denial of me but of the me that gets in the way," says Wilkie Au. The work is also done by simply sitting: letting be. Synchronicity lets us know just when to hold on or let go: a series of losses invites us to let go; a series of opportunities encourages us to take hold. Bears know when to fight, when to claw their way to what they want, and when to lie down and let nature take its course. They do by natural instinct what we do by spiritual attentiveness to synchronicity. Look at the metaphor of hibernation: bears enter a self-dug cave for one to four months with no eating or drinking, since they survive on their own body fat, even recycling their own waste. They awake weighing 25 percent less than they weighed when they lay down. *Can I let that much of my ego go? Will I want to stay in control and refuse ever to lie down?*

There is something sane and awake in us that is shut off when we are struggling through our dramas and holding our ego position in them. This something sane and awake is the transcendent function of the psyche that always comes up with a healing alternative in the form of an image or path that cuts through our dilemmas, no matter how confounding. It comforts us and shows us our inner resources. It comes to life in the gaps between the struggles. We stop to take time out and sit in what is. This is how Buddha sat. We often overvalue the consensual point of view that confirms our ego habits, and thereby automatically reject these gaps or refuse to see them. Creative moments happen when a habitual pattern is interrupted in favor of something altogether new: a gap in the same old story!

The humbling journey through ego is addressed paradoxically in *The Way of Tao:* "Attain the climax of emptiness." When we assent to emptying ourselves of ego, Taoists say that a "mysterious pass through the apparently impenetrable mountains" has been stumbled upon. It opens in the midst of the jagged rocks. It appears where thoughts, fantasies, fears, and desires cease. It is the pause between stimulus and response, where freedom is. It is the pause between our storylines. There we become the fair and alert witnesses and a serene sanity arises in us. This pause/pass is the soul space between ego and Self. It is the heart of me and the soul of the universe, now finally acknowledged as one and the same. In other words, it is the point at which I become and am synchronicity! "After the Way is realized, there is nowhere that is not the mysterious pass," says Ho Yang.

The road is fraught with danger because we are involved in a rite of passage from outside to inside, from the periphery to the center (of the mandala of wholeness), from the profane to the sacred, from the ephemeral to the eternal, from the mortal to the immortal. Immortality means beyond the limits of ego and the conditions of our existence. Attaining this center requires the equivalent of ego death. It is a consecration to and initiation into the sacred, i.e., the discovery of one's spirituality. It is the ultimate answer to the question: why am I here? I am here to live out my destiny "on earth as it is in heaven." This sounds trite at first but look more closely.

"On earth" is the metaphor for my psychological work of building a healthy ego, one that will be an apt instrument for my spiritual work. "In heaven" is the metaphor for the spiritual work of releasing unconditional love, universal wisdom, and heal-ing power into the world. Now look at the three little words that are the bridge between: *as it is.* When I say yes to the "as it is," I create the bridge between earth and heaven, between my psy-chological and spiritual work, between my ego mortality and my immortal destiny!

Ego/Self at a Glance

Our Self is essential, that which is permanent and indestruc-tible in us.

It is our very being.

Our ego is existential, that which is continually changing. It takes the form of action.

Our destiny is to exhibit existentially what is in us essen-tially: letting the light through.

Our work is to display in our ego actions and choices the
eternal design of the Self.

This is what is meant by an axis of ego and Self.

There is essential synchronicity in this aptitude for axis
(individuation) in our psyche.

Existential synchronicity appears in the moment that initiates or furthers the axis work.

Essential synchronicity is in the eternal harmony of ego/Self
and soul/universe.

This is the harmony we discover in meditation.

Existential synchronicity is in the meaningful coincidences
that point our ego to its path.

It is something we notice in our conscious attention to our
life process.

*In late antiquity the major part of what we call today the
psyche was located outside the individual in the animated
matter of the universe; it consisted of a multiplicity of col-
liding components, or of gods, star-divinities, and demons,
or of powers in the organs of the body, or in chemical
substances. Jung has shown that what we now call the collective unconscious has never been something psychological;
it always was relegated to the outside cosmos, to the extra-
psychic cosmic sphere. Man protected himself against it with
religious symbols and rituals in order to avoid experiencing
it within himself. Only today do we discover the collective
unconscious in the area of inner psychic experience. Further-
more, in antiquity, the conscious ego of man was a helpless
victim of different moods or divine influences. Only slowly
did man develop an ethical, critical attitude toward these
powers.*   —Marie-Louise Von Franz, *Psyche and Matter*

Just Coincidence: The Trickster of Ego

A greater power than we can contradict hath thwarted our intents.
— *Romeo and Juliet*

In Tom and Jerry cartoons, Jerry the powerless mouse overcomes and outwits Tom, the powerful cat: the humor is in the reversal of nature's usual arrangement. We see this reversal also in *The Wizard of Oz:* little Dorothy kills the powerful witch. In the Christmas mystery, a helpless infant intimidates the powerful King Herod. Lowly characters humble imperious ones. The trickster is the archetype of that comeuppance. We have certainly noticed in our own lives how persons and events keep coming along to depose our ego's arrogance, to show us how little in control we really are, to strip us of our imaginary entitlements to exemptions from the conditions of existence, to disrupt our best laid schemes. Such people and events are trickster visits to us.

The trickster is the ego demolitions expert who helps us become more realistic about our psychological limitations and ultimately our spiritual limitlessness. He leads us to border crossings where we are tricked into our own wholeness. This is an energy within ourselves and within the universe that humbles us, topples our ego, upsets our plans, demonstrates to us how little our wishes matter, and dissolves the forms that no longer serve us though we may be clinging to them for dear life. Comfort and routine are the two sworn enemies of our lively energy, and the trickster battles these enemies on our behalf.

The trickster is the mythic personification of synchronicity. Within all of us is an instinct to consolidate an axis between ego and Self. To do this requires some deflating of our ego. The trickster is the archetype of that deflation. The trickster in relationship is that man who fooled you, that woman who betrayed you, that predator/partner who used you, took your money, etc. In each instance, someone, something, or some event turned your life upside down or showed you how foolish and vulnerable you were, how you were not all you cracked yourself up to be! Fear and desire are the calisthenics of the trickster ego and the tools to show the ego its inadequacy.

Humor, irony, and paradox are the transformative tools of the trickster, the transpersonal source of wit. A pretty face may be the trickster; alcohol and cocaine are the trickster; romantic attachment is the trickster; the penis is definitely the trickster! All of these absorb our energy and can lead us to desperate addiction and out-of-control behavior. We are fooled into believing that any of these can grant us permanent happiness or increase our personal stature. The trickster makes the same promises that Adam and Eve believed when this whole human enterprise began.

The trickster is the archetype of synchronicity and of illusion and ambiguity. He tricks us out of the status quo and into new perspectives by unruly events that at first seem negative but become positive or at first seem positive and become negative. The trickster archetype is the psyche's answer to oppression and grandiosity. Fearless and uncompromising, it exposes pretension and pomposity wherever we manifest it or fall prey to it. (The joker or fool fulfilled this function for the king in medieval courts.)

Opposites constellate in the psyche. We all contain both arrogance and humility. When we are overly arrogant, the trickster may humble us. He makes our unused, unconscious humility conscious and visible. The trickster fosters wholeness in spite of our ego's objections or resistance. He will not allow one-sidedness but will arrange our circumstances so that our other side will have its chance to emerge. Selfish people may be forced to be selfless; macho men may be forced to be tender. Wholeness often comes into our lives uninvited. The trickster is its escort.

The trickster dupes and is duped, gets into trouble and out of it too, shuffles chance and mischance, shows us our dark side, has irresistible charm, is spontaneous and unpredictable. He is a comic or a jinx who uses art, artifice, sedition, and dishonesty. The trickster appears in unexpectedness, mischief, disorder, shock, amorality. He balances rigid and righteous attitudes with humor and flexibility. He comes to the entrenched to release spontaneity and thus restore psychic balance and latitude, thwarts conscious plans, creates inner and outer upheavals, induces or forces us into new arrangements (things go topsy turvy). The trickster helps deflate the warrior version of heroism in which the object is only to win rather than to live through pain with honor, honesty, and love. The trickster leads us to a primordial dawning consciousness of order from dissonance. He devours ego, unites opposites, and thereby transforms, meaninglessness into meaning-fulness, predicament into path, sterile voids into fertile pastures, stuckness into a way out, and even death into life.

The trickster is Puck, Ariel, poltergeists, the Joker, the devil — a rascal and a prankster but not a scoundrel. Dionysus is the trick-ster when he grants greedy Midas's wish. He is the oldest of all mythic characters, hence the Crow and Blackfoot see him as the "Old Man." His longevity is explained by the liveliness of the stories about him and our fascination with them: "So stubborn a refusal to forget could not be an accident," says Paul Radin, referring to the trickster. In other cultures, he is a rabbit, raven, coyote, spider, monkey, or the plumed serpent. He is the clever animal who helps in time of need and upsets the plans of those who think they have no needs.

In our culture, the trickster has appeared as the Cheshire cat, Bugs Bunny, Daffy Duck. In Greek mythology, he is Hermes, god of synchronicity, who meets us with lucky chances and windfalls as well as the "psychopomp" who guides us to the ego-slaying underworld (our own unconscious). As a god of ambiguity, he invented language which explains *and* hides: hermeneutics and hermetic! He is the messenger between the ego world and the world of the Self, the God of revelation who manifests spirit in matter, showing how matter matters. He is the god of alchemy cooking up the precious from the useless. Since he was born at night in a cave, he can see at night, i.e., he can see our shadow and show us how to capitalize on it. Zeus gave him the task/

gift of bringing souls to Hades and back again. He is thus the mediator who bridges the gap between life and death. It was he who brought Persephone back from the underworld. Hermes is the personification of the unconscious, of prime matter, and of the power to hold all the opposites, material and spiritual. He is the artificer of individuation — the consummation of personal wholeness. So much of our destiny is all in the humorous hands of this trickster!

How the Trickster Visits

He has pulled down the mighty from their thrones; he has exalted the lowly.   —Luke 1:52

- A treasure is lost or found: I have powers or riches but am tricked out of them by promises or misplaced trust and thereby lose them, e.g., the young man who leaves his gold in the keeping of the dishonest innkeeper.
- I am humiliated by being bested by someone I thought was less than myself in skill or intelligence, e.g., the tortoise and hare or my showing off at bat and then being struck out by a rookie pitcher.
- I am planning to quit in a huff when I am fired.
- I am shown to be quite fragile by my overreaction to a practical joke or a rejection.
- I am shocked to realize my partner is using the time I am off having an affair to have one herself.
- I think I am really loved by someone who only wants my money.
- While engaged, I fall head over heels in love with someone who does not reciprocate. The whole experience shows me how little in love I was with my fiancée.
- A visit from the trickster happens most often through personal crisis. This corresponds to the dismemberment experience

of the hero, i.e., the dismantling of ego: we are broken up, we are forced to let go. Through such symbolic death we are re-born and descend to the underworld to converse with sages and shamans and then ascend to converse with gods. It is like the rope trick in which the body ascends, falls to the ground in pieces, and is reassembled. But remember what Pliny said when he saw the colossus of Rhodes in broken pieces on the ground after an earthquake: "Even in pieces it was a wonder of the world!"

 ## PRACTICE

In each of the above listings, try to locate the positive and negative hidden parts of yourself. Identify in the list of trickster visits above the ones that have hap-pened to you and how you handled them. How do they entrench or release you? How would humor have changed your experience of trickster visits? Who are the people or events or circumstances in your life that have served as tricksters? How have you been a trickster to others?

If you are seriously willing to work with trickster energy, try the following:

- Noticing what you are feeling or sensing right now

- Saying yes to what is, like it or not

- Allowing things to remain topsy-turvy for a day longer than you can stand

- Not looking for soft landings but allowing yourself to land on concrete reality

- Attending to the lunar, unexpected world

- Welcoming crisis as ego deflation: your coziness has been addressed, processed, and resolved by the universe!

- Inviting the pain of change rather than avoiding it

- Having a sense of humor, being satisfied with less self-importance, and "playing with your pain" (Charlie Chaplin's way of describing the secret of the success of his comedies).

- Inventing rituals that take you out of character — as happens on Halloween, Mardi Gras, April Fool's Day

- Going out of character: exploring very different lifestyles or belief systems, trying entirely new interests or careers, changing personal style and choices, e.g., from fear-based to courage-based, from tight to loose, from inhibited to experimental, from no to yes.

We don't have to struggle to be free. Absence of struggle is freedom.
                                                          — Chogyam Trungpa

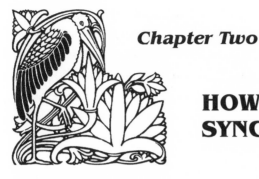

Chapter Two

HOW TO SEE
SYNCHRONICITY

There are many events in the womb of time which will be delivered.
— *Othello*

Synchronicity is the strikingly meaningful coincidence of two events or of a series of events. It can also be the coincidence of a psychic perception and a simultaneously occurring event, as happens in ESP. Premonitions are in this category. In both ESP and premonition, the case can be made for synchronicity only if meaningfulness is present. This is always the ultimate criterion of synchronicity.

An example of synchronous premonition is given by Jung about a patient of his with many phobias. All were cleared in therapy except for one: fear of outdoor stairs. The patient was later killed by a stray bullet from a street fight on just such stairs. This was synchronicity, a premonition of a significant truth — not a phobia after all. (Or perhaps the phobia was a long-standing self-protective device!)

Synchronicity occurs in a dream that reveals what is already true or about to become true: Lincoln dreamed he was as-sassinated one week before the event. Dreams and astrology manifest many synchronous correspondences. There is immense synchronicity in the zodiac and in our inclinations or choices. Rituals are forms of synchronicity in that they are outward enactments of corresponding inward graces.

Synchronicity appears in our work on ourselves. There may be synchronicity in the fact that our knowledge of our real issues — in ourselves and in our relationships — comes simultaneously with the strength to face them. We are usually in denial for a long time before we finally recognize and acknowledge our own truth. Synchronicity is in the fact that we often only let ourselves know when we can deal with what we know.

Our inner healers — the physician, psychologist, and priestly guide we met in the prologue — work synchronously in providing resources tailored to our needs. We join in synchronously when we use the skills that correlate to this natural inclination and make it one cooperative rendezvous of grace and effort. We match our daily skills to the healing course of action always and already in progress in the self-restorative psyche. The practices in this book engender those skills. It is in your hands now because the time for it to speak to you — and raise your hopes in yourself — has come. In these recent years we have noticed a plethora of books on angels, on inner child work, on codependency, on recovery. As the population is ready to address its need, the teachers arrive with their books in hand. May this be one for you.

Déjà vu is the illusory belief that something happening in the present was already experienced in the past. (If it indeed happened, it is a memory, not déjà vu.) It is synchronicity when it represents a meaningful connection to a past moment that is still unfinished in our psyches and now suddenly makes a plea for our attention. Events, enterprises, and relationships register in our psyches with the simple vocabulary of ants: done or undone? Undone in the human context means still unaddressed, or unprocessed, or unresolved. An experience of déjà vu may point us to that context and invite us to explore the site where a construction is still incomplete. The overarching yearning for wholeness in our psyches is the genus of these specific and immediate longings for conclusion.

There is synchronicity in the events of the day that create a strong reaction in us: they are metaphors for deeper unacknowledged feelings and unfinished emotional business that may be calling for attention. For example: I was very upset about being behind a school bus in traffic today. This may be a metaphor for something holding up the traffic of my life journey.

Sometimes words prove to be true in a larger sense than ever we intended: "Little did I know then!" We may state something humorously or figuratively and if we think about it more carefully, we realize it has precisely that meaning literally. For instance, you ask me how my stormy relationship is going and I say, "Things are sort of patched up." Later, I find myself returning to that phrase and realize that it describes the very nature of my relationship: things are never resolved or changed, only patched up. I have opened myself to my own truth by a Freudian slip of synchronicity.

Synchronicity is in the coincidence of an image held on to with fascination over the years and some piece of our work on ourselves for which it is a metaphor. Anything that has gripped and enriched us is implicated in our destiny. If all my life I have been in awe of the shapes and subtleties of seashells, there is probably a lesson or an assistance (physical, psychological, or spiritual) that will come to me precisely at the time I need it from the presence or image of shells. Dostoevsky says: "It must have lain hidden in my soul, though I knew nothing of it, and it rose suddenly to my memory when it was needed." Images held on to with fascination are assisting forces. Blisses are too. "When you follow your bliss," Joseph Campbell says, "doors open where there were no doors before!" That is synchronicity. And, when bliss meets talent, behold the synchronicity of finding a vocation!

When we are ready to learn, a teacher appears. This is synchronicity. Occasionally, a person who died long ago or recently comes to mind over and over in the course of a week or more. It could be that the meaning of that person in our life is coming home to us in a compelling way. Perhaps we learned something from that person and need to remember it now. Perhaps there is something we are now ready to learn. This may be another form of synchronicity. The face of the teacher or the grandfather appears when the time has come to be instructed or to gain a deeper insight into who we are. This might even be the time to ask that person to be our guide from the other world if that fits our worldview.

A related example of synchronicity is in the experience of something that we have always wanted, a goal in life. What makes us want something so fervently and for so long is its just-right synchronous consonance with the needs of our fellow humans. What we want so fervently is what the world needs from us so urgently. Our personal goal will become a wider resource. An alignment of personal and universal purposes is a beautiful example of how synchronicity and destiny go hand in hand. The mountainous desires in our hearts are the desires of the everlasting hills of the world. Enthusiasm means, after all, being filled with the divine. We can also tell that we are on track to our destiny because the closer we come to it, the more it absorbs us. We become more committed than ever to living out our needs and wishes and tailoring them to our life's goal. This is the kind of committedness that frees us from fear of the world. We feel at home in it, co-workers with it: "My soul: world soul: divine soul: one synchronous and sonorous reality."

Acting consciously in accord with an unconscious readiness, though without planning, is an example of synchronicity, e.g., as I am in a letting-go phase, losses happen. In my challenge phase, opportunities and oppositions happen. To integrate is to go with what wants to happen: not stopping the momentum of that which I cannot change but riding it, jumping on the train as it comes through the station. Trust is always an invaluable companion on the synchronous track. Our work is then to make conscious choices that match inner, unconscious momentum. This is the readiness that is all, referred to by Shakespeare.

There is synchronicity in the fact that each of us has just the right gifts and talents that the world needs in our lifetime. The Class of 1998 is made up of members who, taken together, have everything the world needs for it to evolve fully now. Some of our classmates are models and heroes and some are rogues and rascals. Some are getting A's in their work and some are failing. Some love their alma mater and others are attempting to destroy her. As a member of this class, I have a unique contribution that no one else can make but me. I am an indispensable participant in the vast unfolding and protecting of my world. Among those alive this year, there is a precise and ample combination of ingredients and strengths for the nourishment of today's world. Will I add my pinch of salt? What holds me back from giving the gifts I was born to give? How can I doubt that I have a part to play in this arc of wholeness that moves in such perfect timing toward the eternal commencement? The other people in my life and on the planet now have come to receive my gifts. They are assisting forces in my self-discovery and self-sharing.

Synchronicity also occurs in looking back upon your life and seeing how it all prepared you or instructed you for the fullest fruition of your potential. A hidden feeling or truth waited to be awakened by just the right person or circumstance, sometimes painfully. My destiny had to have just such a beginning. My neglectful father helped me practice for the independent life I live now. My empty cupboard helped me care about starving children. James Hillman writes: "This way of seeing removes the burden from the early years as having been a mistake and yourself a victim of handicaps and cruelties; instead it is the acorn in the mirror."

Everyone and every event in life's drama is part of the metaphor of our journey. The issue from an old relationship may not be: "how bad he was" but: "how much I needed to learn!" Most of us keep meeting partners who show us exactly where our work is, e.g., men who abuse, women who are unfaithful. The wounds are openings into our missing life. Often, the only way a lost piece of ourselves or of our history comes back to us is through another person. The unknown is scary, *so people and events come along that help us go there.* This is synchronicity. The only mistake we make is hanging on to some people too long or too briefly. *How and with whom did I do that?* We take them as literally themselves instead of as themselves *and* metaphorical forces, come to boost or chide. *What delivered me from the constrictions into the open air? Who finally pointed the way beyond my limitations?*

There is a special synchronicity in suddenly saying yes to an offer or experience that would ordinarily be out of character for us to assent to. We break through an inhibition or a fear and suddenly we find ourselves in a new, unexplored world. And lo, this new realm accurately reflects our deepest needs and wishes. A whole new chapter opens in our lives because of a chance change. The yes to something that anytime before would have received a no was synchronicity within us taking us beyond our limits to our destiny. Whoever made the original invitation was an assisting force.

Along the path we meet an army of afflicting forces and gather a family of assisting forces. "We meet those to whom we belong in the world of the Self," says Von Franz. We meet people who show us the parts of ourselves that we have refused to acknowledge and integrate into our own lives. These discredited features of ourselves are both positive and negative (shadow sides of us). There is synchronicity in how we unerringly find exactly the people who show us to ourselves. *Who comes to mind?*

Events occur that provide the same service. If *this* is happening to me, it can be one of the ingredients of my destiny! The only thing that can get in the way is my own ego, not the events that occur or the people that bring them. A coup of grace brought me here! "Someday it will help to remember even this," Virgil wrote about a sad event. *What about my story, my events?*

Therapists may especially relate to the above two paragraphs. Clients seem to appear presenting just the issues that we ourselves most need to work on. Teachers are asked just the questions they may need to ask themselves. Writers may be writing just what they most need to attend to. *As all three of these, I know all this is true for me!*

Finally, there is synchronicity in divination devices such as the *I Ching* or the tarot: one ineluctably chooses the hexagram or card that coincides with one's circumstance. This meaningful coincidence is based on the belief that the psyche will direct us to the exact information that we need when we need it.

The *I Ching* is the ancient Chinese "Book of Changes." It is a resource text that one turns to with questions about one's journey, and it works entirely by synchronicity. The inquirer throws coins that lead to the section of the book that speaks precisely and accurately to his or her situation. The philosophy of the *I Ching* states that all human affairs are governed by a single law: change. This inclination toward change has a geometry: it displays itself in sixty-four processes in the form of graphic hexagrams. When our personal choices align with these processes, harmony results between us and the ensouled universe and we are living out our destiny. In this Chinese approach to reality, the locus of the mutability is the center of the universe. This center is perfectly still; yet from it ripple out the many and constant changes we see. It is the same center as that of the mandala: a oneness that allows, generates, and transcends duality. The *I Ching* is one of the most powerful of the ancient examples of synchronicity. It is entirely based on the belief that coincidence is instructive and that the psyche will direct us to the exact information that we need when we need it. The book/process is a resource of the soul, since it addresses the point at which conscious and unconscious meet. When Jung met Richard Wilhelm, who translated the *I Ching*, he worked more earnestly on the idea of synchronicity.

The tarot is a pack of twenty-two major cards (corresponding to the letters of the Hebrew alphabet) plus a joker/fool. The cards depict archetypal and alchemical figures, virtues, and metaphors that were originally meant to be contemplated and studied. In the seventeenth century, they became pointers to where human fortunes lie. The figures appear in this order in the deck: minstrel, archpriestess, empress, emperor, archpriest, lover, chariot, justice, hermit, wheel of fortune, strength, the hanged man, death, temperance, devil, tower struck by lightning, stars, moon, sun, judgment, world, and finally or first: the fool. The cards present an image of the path to destiny through initiation. The gold suit stands for the material forces in the world, the scepter represents the power of authority; the chalice is for sacrifice, and the sword represents the dispensing of justice. In each suit there is a king, queen, knight, and knave (jack) representing the categories of earthly power. Scepters stand for government; swords represent the military; a chalice indicates the priesthood; and the gold is for intellectual and aesthetic pursuits. Cards one through eleven lead us on the solar way: active, conscious, masculine. Cards twelve through twenty-two show the lunar way: passive, unconscious, feminine. Each image combines the inner and outer world in the context of human experience. The intention of the deck is to present a full panoply of the archetypal possibilities in every human being and show us the immediate turn of the road to the activation of those potentials. The tarot is an album of pictures of us. Each of us is the tarot.

Astrology is another rich source of synchronicity in its study of the direct and meaningful coincidence between the layout of the stars and the blueprint of our lives. The Zodiac ("circle of animals") contains twelve symbols that indicate the terrestrial situation when the sun is in a particular part of the sky: Aries: the ram, spring; Taurus: growth of plants and mating of animals; Gemini: proliferation of life within an ecological whole; Cancer: crab, sap of life flows copiously; Leo: the sun's fiery power; Virgo: harvest and seed for the next year; Libra: autumnal equinox, turns into Scorpio: the sign of death. Sagittarius, the archer of reflection, since he looks back as he rides into the winter solstice. Capricorn: fish tail and goat body representing a transition from old to new as the sun climbs again; Aquarius: water-pourer appearing as rains come in winter; Pisces: living but hidden growth beneath the watered earth, preceding Aries and lilac spring again.

"I find my zenith doth depend upon a most auspicious star, whose influence / If now I count not, but omit, my fortunes will ever after droop," says Shakespeare in *The Tempest*. There is synchronicity in astrology, since our psyche is mirrored in the night sky of our birth and our unfolding life. The unconscious indeed contains planets (gods) as archetypes. All the planets together make up the unconscious, which is a pageant of archetypal figures familiar from all the stories we have read and resonated to Mars: hero; Jupiter: king; Venus: female anima-soul; Uranus: male animus-spirit; Saturn: father, conservator; Mercury: trickster; Moon: persona; Sun: individuation. *Body, heart, and mind correspond to pairings of gods:* body: Mercury and Venus; emotions: Mars and Jupiter; Mind: Saturn and Uranus.

In medieval times, St. Albert the Great, inspired by the Persian mystic Ibn Sina, said that the psyche has the power to alter external matter and things when it is in highly charged emotional states and when a favorable astrological pattern coincides with it. For the year to be complete and for nature to work, all the signs are necessary. Likewise all humanity requires all the signs for the wholeness of the human community. (A jury originally was made up of twelve men, each with a different astrological sign for fairness and complete human amplitude in judgment.)

The psyche is indeed a solar system: instincts, emotions, and thoughts orbit the luminaries of the Self and ego. The sun represents consciousness and moon the unconscious. They are the inner and outer faces of the human psyche. The planets are operational principles of action, heart, and mind. Heaven and earth have definite connections: our blood flow and coagulation correlate with the moon, as do the tides of the ocean. "As above, so below" is the medieval alchemical way of saying this. Uranus represents breaking away from the familiar to embrace the new. It is thus the planet that represents synchronicity. Uranus is the divine intervention that introduces unexpected changes and reversals through unusual people and events that meet us on our path. *Can I meet the unexpected with nothing but space between it and me?*

"Look how the floor of heaven is thick inlaid with patens of bright gold...such harmony is in immortal souls!" The human psyche contains all the stars and planets as metaphors of our full potential. They are not only heavenly bodies but macrocosms of our individual microcosm. We are composed of and highly responsive to their every orbit and vibration. We respond because we are made in their image. The heavens *mirror* us and we are truly children of the stars: terrestrial reflections of celestial constellations: "Rejoice that your names are written in heaven."

 PRACTICE

• There is a story in me that wants to be told. I come to know the story by contemplating the events of my life. It takes work to allow myself to see clearly, and the work reveals me to myself. We have the potential in us for truth about ourselves and the world. When we are compelled by obligatory or fearful inclinations we are caught in deadly energy. When we are impelled by blissful *choices* we are liberated by lively energy. *Which of my choices this week are based on obligation or fear and which flow from bliss?*

• All of us also have a myth (a driving force in life) in common: the heroic journey. A personal myth is our unique way to make this happen. "What will die with me when I die, what pathetic if fragile form will the world lose?" Borges asked. What is the driving force of my life? What would I dedicate myself to without reserve? What grounds me? Am I living out a myth that is tailored to the best that is in me?

• Has there been a series of similar events — or dreams — in the past month or two? What is the common theme? What force beyond yourself is trying to reach you through this orchestration of your life? What challenge does this theme present to you? What is exciting about it? What scares you? Write out the answers to these questions and notice which feelings arise in you. How do these feelings help or hinder you in responding to the theme?

• Most people have some powers of premonition or ESP. When have they displayed themselves in the course of your life? For most people, they arise more emphatically when something is brewing within. Do you notice yourself becoming more sensitive when major changes or transitions are afoot? The more attention you pay to the powers — no matter how minor — the more they will increase. Inner power is a guest that loves to visit a welcoming host.

• List the things you are finding out about yourself from this book and from the synchronicities of your recent life. For instance, if a series of losses has occurred, has it been difficult or easy to grieve and let go? Usually, when we are ready to know where our work is, we are ready to begin doing it. The work consists of addressing, processing, and, hopefully, thereby resolving what has come up. As you move through this book, you will be gathering skills that will help you in that enterprise. Begin today by reading your list aloud and saying: "Yes, this did happen. Yes, I have something to learn from it. Yes, I am willing to stay focused on this and to feel the feelings that come up around it." Even if you are not ready to do all this today, you are beginning the process, and having that beginner's mind alone is success. Form an image of your inner psychologist and your inner guide and ask their assistance in the ongoing project of living a more and more conscious and self-expanding life.

• The next time you experience déjà vu, ask what is unfinished that is asking for closure, or what loss you are regretting, or what era of life you might like to return to in order to begin again at that point. How does any of this elicit grief or its milder friend: nostalgia?

• If you are familiar with the *I Ching,* tarot, or astrology, consult these forms of divination at the most touching or compelling moments of your work with this book. Take what you receive as a gift that synchronously accelerates your progress on your personal path.

• Notice the negating phrases of your parents that you keep

hearing in your head and those you say most often to your children or partner. How are these true in a larger sense than is found in the literal meaning? How do these *sentences* dictate your life choices, your manner with others, and your self-image? How can they be redesigned so that they are healing? What are the positive hurrahs you heard in childhood and the ones you say to others now?

• What you have wanted to be all your life may be synchronous with what the universe needs from you to fulfill your destiny of happiness and the capacity to give to others what only you can give. What has held you back from going for it? What has propelled you toward it? Thank the people who encouraged your self-emergence. Let yourself feel anger toward those who interfered with your achievement of your life goals. What will it take for you to let go of blame and shame and to move on under your own steam? Are you saying to yourself that it is too late? If you are, picture Grandma Moses now and tell her that in your mind. She began painting in her seventies and died at one hundred and one!

Synchronicity and Mirroring

> *Only in the arms of someone can the first "I am" be pronounced, or rather, risked.*   — D. W. Winnicott

A profoundly personal form of synchronicity is in mirroring: congruent and gracious acceptance of an infant by a mother. The infant has precisely the needs that the mother can instinctually fulfill. Such mirroring installs a coherent sense of self, i.e., healthy, functional ego identity. There is synchronicity in this arrangement in nature since mothers instinctively articulate in mirroring what babies need for self-articulation. Resourceful children, whose parents were inadequate or neglectful about mirroring, found their own sources of mirroring in relatives, other adults, older siblings, etc.

Mirroring is unconditional positive regard shown by attention, acceptance, affection, and allowing. Our self-esteem and self-respect originate in the holding environment in early childhood: it emerges from a mirroring dialogue. Why do we fear abandonment so much? It is the withdrawal of mirroring: a necessity if we are to survive emotionally.

The opposite of this kind of respecting is shaming. This is why the more ashamed we are about ourselves, the less self-respect we tend to have. Shame was installed where respect belonged. Shame is self-abandonment. We are then wounded in ways that someday it will be our work to heal. Hopefully, we will feel compassion for the same wounds in others. Self-respect is self-mirroring and leads to love in return toward those who mirror us.

Some of our feelings are felt as dangerous to others and their mirroring powers are then limited. People may, for instance, mirror our grief when our partner dies or leaves. They mirror the immediate sadness, anger, and fear that grief evokes. But a few months later, as we delve into the deeper and much more threatening depths of our grief, we may feel isolated because no one wants to go down there with us. Only very true and strong friends or therapists may be willing to be with us in that part of the agony. *Who has accompanied me all the way to the bottom of the pit of myself? Have I ever thanked that person? Have I been willing to make that trip with others?*

In mirroring, I succeed in seeing myself through another's empathic attunement to me. This gives me a sense of effectiveness and competence, and my self-esteem increases. Accurate mirroring of feelings in early life — and later — leads to a comfortable body image and a strong sense of myself. A clear, cohesive, stable sense of self is thus formed by a series of mirroring experiences.

If the original mirroring bond was lacking, I can find the missing psychic structures later in life in new persons who help me shore up or build my own crumbling structures. This is how relationships vitalize me. The depleted is filled; the fragmented is unified; the broken is repaired. The resultant sense of mastery also increases my self-esteem and gives me a sense of continuity and power. In healthy development, I increase my capacity to internalize nurturance, and it forms reliable and ineradicable structures in my psyche that replace the marred or fragmentary ones. The ultimate purpose and outcome of mirroring is to develop self-mirroring skills. This is the self-empathy that expands into compassion for others.

When we are synchronously mirrored, the circuits for our emotions are reinforced, since the brain uses the same pathways to generate an emotion as to respond to one. To reciprocate an emotion is to reinforce the capacity to feel it again, and safely too. This is why once we are free to feel, we can feel more deeply for others. Our destiny is given a boost when we have received healthy mothering or have found a mirroring dialogue with other adults later.

Personal human evolution occurs in the transition from a restriction to original family members for nurturance to a new support system of enriching people found in the wider world, a new family. A healthy person is never without such a set of ties, established through a series of synchronous meetings and relationships. Adult psychological health is not independence but interdependence: resatellizing around healthy providers of mirroring. Usually, for this to happen, we have to have embarked upon our own work on ourselves first.

Sometimes we feel unsupported by others. An image in nature sheds light on this condition: alder bushes grow on rocky ledges around glaciers, unsupported by soil. They fertilize themselves from air with nitrogen! Each leaf that falls in autumn richly fertilizes the ground with this nitrogen and lays the groundwork for an alder forest that will appear in the future. When our environment offers no nourishment, we have to have this same skill of finding what we need from thin air! To find it is grace. Emily Dickinson describes it: "Something [in us] adjusts itself to midnight." Our very identity is a cycle of seasons, a dawn following a darkness, a high tide following a low ebb, a rainbow following a storm, a getting up following a falling down. Our human enterprise has such an undemanding elegance!

In mirroring, one person reflects another's inner feelings. Such synchronous attunement leads to a core self, which for us humans is the same as core relatedness. "Feeling states that are never attuned to will be experienced only alone, isolated from the interpersonal context of shareable experience. What is at stake here is nothing less than the shape of and the extent of the shareable inner universe," writes Daniel Stern.

A feature of this personal synchronicity is revealed in the choices we make in relationship. Sometimes we uncannily find the very person who can mirror us. Sometimes we find someone who will throw us back on our own resources to mirror ourselves. Often we will try so poignantly to wrest from an inadequate partner the need fulfillment we originally missed. We find and attach ourselves to the very person who will recreate the original scenarios of our injured childhood. Our wish to repeat is as strong as our wish to recover!

A person's power to fascinate or engage us may be in the perfect fit that person provides for us to see where our own wounds — and/or potentialities — are. This is double synchronicity. "I may find hidden corners of my psychic housed in you. I may see the deeper lineaments of my own unfaced face. Some people hit the target of who I am and of where my work is. Some hit the bull's-eye and my addiction or attachment grows accordingly." A liberation happens when the other is not taken literally but as a metaphor of our own past and our deep-buried yearnings for wholeness. Others can exhume us; it is up to us to rise again.

The wounds of our past are reopened in our adult relationships because our destiny is partly derived from our wounds! Synchronicity points us toward our destiny precisely because something in us needs healing. The wound of being unloved invites us to a destiny of compassion for ourselves and for those who feel as bereft as we.

We think we want love and closeness but when we see how love can bring back our old hurts and fears, we pull back. Actually, we really want love only when we are willing to take all it brings. If our relationship is painful, we may make it more tolerable by attenuating it: becoming wrapped up in external, practical concerns, becoming combative, having an affair, focusing on work or children to the exclusion of a partner. This is how we protect ourselves from feeling the archaic throbs of pain that are revived in adult intimacy. To choose to process the early issues of our life by grieving and resolving them is therefore a choice for intimacy.

The unfulfilled needs of childhood — attention, affection, acceptance, and allowing us to be ourselves — remain dead and alive in us all our lives. They are dead in that we missed out on their fulfillment. That calls for grieving and letting go. They are alive as challenges: to give nurturance to ourselves and to find it moderately in healthy partners. The synchronicity is in the intersection of these forces in our lives and in the discovery of two corresponding boons: finding out how to do the griefwork of our inner child and finding a partner who is wholesome enough to cooperate with us in need fulfillment. The former is found in self-help books, therapy, and intuition. The latter is serendipity. An apt partner comes unsought when we neither seek nor avoid and when time grants its benediction. The right partner will be someone who has grieved his or her own past and is now ready for sane love. That person will say: "What synchronicity to have found *you!*"

How comforting it might have been to know that one was not alone in one's flaws and vulnerabilities, and to feel assured of one's place despite everything.
— Robert Haren, "Shame," *Atlantic Monthly,* Feb. 1992

PRACTICE

I look long and honestly at my childhood and at the relationships that have been important to me throughout my life and ask myself which ones mirrored me. Is the relationship I am in now one that mirrors me? Am I mirroring others? Do I show love by an unconditional acceptance, affection, attention, and allowing the other to be himself?

I take an inventory of all my relationships: What do I appreciate in each of them? What is still unresolved? Do I owe any amends to anyone? If so, I choose to make them if it seems appropriate and would not cause harm. How has each relationship shown me how to love more? How has each one opened my heart? Do I keep my heart closed now and blame it on a former partner?

A heart that is opening rivals any flower that blooms!

Tales That Tell

Synchronicity appears in a single, sometimes painful, occurrence that sets off a chain of events that leads us to our destiny:

Joseph in the Old Testament was sold into slavery to the Egyptians by his brothers. He rose in power in Egypt because of his skill in dream interpretation and personal integrity. In accord with his interpretation of the Pharaoh's dream, he prepared for and headed off a disaster from a future famine. When his brothers, many years later, felt the effects of this same famine, they came to Joseph and he was able to feed them and be reconciled with his family.

Synchronicity is found in an event that seems meaningless when it happens but later shows itself to be of utmost significance:

Abraham Lincoln, out of compassion for a man who was forced to sell all he had, bought a barrel from him for his asking price of one dollar. Lincoln never asked what it contained. He stored it at home and forgot about it. Later on, Lincoln went through a long period of confusion and indecision about whether to enter the legal profession or journalism. In the midst of this quandary, he happened to notice the barrel and lackadaisically opened it. It contained a set of law books. He took this as a sign and entered the profession that led to politics and the presidency. The many synchronicities in Lincoln's life — and in the lives of most great people — show emphatically that synchronicity points to destiny.

Synchronicity is in the concurrence of a dream and a dayworld question or in a dream as a foretelling of the future:

Elias Howe, in the nineteenth century, invented the sewing machine. However, the one thing he could not figure out was how to shape the needle to let the thread run through it and through the material being sewed. He pondered long and hard with no results. Without such a needle, the invention was useless. One night, the man in Massachusetts dreamed he was in Africa and saw natives with strange spears. He observed the unusual shape of the blades: an oblong hole in the center. When Howe awoke, he realized he had found the answer to his question.

Synchronicity shows itself in sudden or spontaneous decisions that we make, not knowing why, that later prove important to our destiny:

Fritz Perls, the founder of Gestalt therapy, taught in a university in Germany in the 1930s. He and two of his colleagues were asked one day by their department chair if any one of them would like a transfer to teach at the German university in South Africa. The two colleagues began asking questions about the practical aspects of the move, but Perls immediately and simply said yes. All three of them were Jewish, and within a few short years, the two colleagues were in concentration camps and Fritz remained safe. Later, he came to America and made his important contribution to the field of psychotherapy.

Synchronicity shows itself in preparations we make to nurture or protect ourselves before we realize we need it:

In his own childhood, Jesse turned often to the Virgin Mary as a mother who would listen to him and nurture him when he could not find these qualities at home. In late 1985, Jesse replaced many of the pictures hanging in his house. It was not until early 1986, when his wife suddenly left him, that Jesse noticed that he had placed a Renaissance picture of the Madonna in every room. One of the pictures was even on the wall beside Jesse as his wife was telling him she was leaving. Jesse must have guessed at what was coming and lined up his support from his familiar — and ever-loyal — female advocate.

Synchronicity occurs in an unusual coincidence that later proves to be necessary or helpful:

In Nebraska, a few years ago, every member of a church choir failed to show up for choir practice on the very night the furnace blew up. Their lives were saved by this unusual coincidence of absence in a group that, prior to that night, appeared faithfully and punctually every week.

Synchronicity can appear as a response to a question about the future or about the reality of a spiritual world:

One evening Concetta, a middle-aged woman whose mother had died recently, was sitting in the house where she had grown up. Her husband would be coming later to pick her up to return to her own house. Concetta was reminiscing about her mother and wondered if there were a heaven and if she would see her there. Suddenly, she found herself saying, "Ma, if there is another world, send me a slice of pizza." Shortly thereafter, Concetta's husband called to tell her he would not be able to pick her up but that her brother would come instead. She said, "That's fine," and was about to hang up when Guido added, "And, by the way, he's bringing you a slice of pizza."

Synchronicity can appear as a string of similar experiences that show us where we may be one-sided and where our work on ourselves may be:

Within one week, the following happened to the macho Roland: his girlfriend left him; his best woman friend became angry at him; his sister did not call him as she said she would; two women did not return his phone calls. All this happened to the man whose mother abandoned him again and again in childhood. This series of rejections by women in such a short time depressed Roland. The depression brought him into contact with his own anima, i.e., his feminine side. He found himself looking at and soon dealing with these issues: his abandonment of his own feminine side, his manner with women, and his fear of showing his softness.

Synchronicity is in the sudden remembrance of a personal history or a series of events that reveals you to yourself or points to the next step of a path you are contemplating:

George was left by Martha on the grounds that he was not committed enough in their six-year relationship. Now, a year later, George is wondering if he really is cut out for a live-in intimate relationship. He is ruminating about this when suddenly the whole history of his relationships flashes before him. George is astounded to realize, for the first time, that every partner of his had the same complaint that Martha had and that he himself often felt uncomfortable with closeness and asked for more "space." At the same time, he has a strong felt sense that intimate bonding is not what he really wants and that the configuration of lighter relationships and deeper friendships feels more appropriate to who he is and has always been. George suddenly realizes that he has been following an imposed ideal by default rather than a preferred reality by choice. He knows intuitively that this new perspective is more appropriately calibrated to his authentic wishes and needs. It feels right to him in the same way that it felt right to him to switch to oatmeal in the morning rather than to continue with bacon and eggs. George will now examine other areas of his life and ask: "Am I acting in accord with the reality of me or am I just doing what I always did or what everyone else does?" The arrival into George's mind of the two cogent pointers — his historical record and his felt sense — precisely as he was facing his dilemma has become the spur of the moment and is thus synchronicity.

Synchronicity appears in the fact that we choose life partners who bring up precisely the issues from our childhood past that have been waiting to be addressed so that we can lay our unfinished business to rest:

Sharon was brought up in a household with a severely abusive father. His message both explicitly and implicitly was: "You don't have what it takes to please me." No matter what she did, Sharon could never do it right in her father's eyes. He belittled her efforts and physically and emotionally abused her throughout her stormy and unhappy childhood. To get out of the house, Sharon married at a young age. After eight years of marriage and two children, her husband, Eric, began having an affair with Grace, a colleague at work. Sharon was devastated by this turn of events, especially since Eric was moving out, refusing to end the affair or even go to therapy to deal with the impact of his actions on the family. She asked him what he found in Grace that he could not find in her. Eric said that she could make love the way he had always wanted it, that she could respond to his needs before he even expressed them, that she could make him feel young and desirable, and that she even kept house better than Sharon!

The familiar ring to these complaints about her struck Sharon like a gong from hell. Once again, she could not please a man. Another woman could, and apparently without much effort. Her anger at Eric saved her from doing what she would have done before: try to figure out new ways to please him. Instead, Sharon went to therapy on her own and learned not to take any of this story literally. This was not about getting Eric back or hating him for what he was doing. Something much more profound was afoot: a metaphor of her own past, a retelling of her unfinished story, an invitation to do her work on herself. The little girl who could not please Daddy was finally getting her chance to tell her opprobrious tale and be done with it.

Sharon became stronger over the succeeding months as she finally grieved the abuses of her woebegone past and learned to take care of herself — and to let go of the need to please men. When Eric's affair with Grace ended and he wanted to come back home, Sharon insisted on his fulfilling two conditions: he would have to work on the relationship in therapy and he would have to become an adult who could appreciate her contribution to his happiness and make a contribution to hers. Eric's affair was the spur for Sharon's liberation from her past and from her bondage to its frustrating and self-defeating reenactment. Grace had indeed visited Sharon's psyche and unlocked its cell door, never to be locked again by any man.

Synchronicity occurs in the delicate balance of prayer and the response to it. This balance is especially evident when we give up our efforts and our attachment to outcomes and we notice the sudden arrival of serendipitous grace:

Maria was frustrated that at age thirty she still had not met the man of her dreams. She asked a priest for advice about how to find a suitable man to marry. "Your name tells you whom to pray to: St. Joseph, spouse of Mary and patron of women who want to find good husbands!" Maria bought a statue of St. Joseph and prayed to him each morning and night for three months with no luck. Even more frustrated and now in despair, she became angry one day and threw the statue out the window. Within a few minutes, there was a knock on her door. Maria opened it and met the man she married a year later. No one was surprised at the name of their first son!

When half gods go, the gods arrive.   — Ralph Waldo Emerson

It is synchronicity when an image that has remained dormant in our imagination over the years suddenly and unexpectedly faces us with a meaning that appears at precisely the moment when it is most useful:

Dominic lived in California and had a fig tree outside his bedroom window. One morning in early fall, he was awakened by the crows complaining about the fact that the figs were all gone. As he lay in bed, he suddenly remembered something from his childhood in Connecticut. At precisely this season, the Italian men in his neighborhood carefully, almost tenderly, wrapped the branches of their fig trees with cloths and covered the trees with blankets and tar paper so that they could survive the harsh winter. Dominic thought spontaneously: "If only they had shown that kind of caring to us kids!" The image of the wrapped tree had never crossed his mind until this moment, let alone this significance.

Dominic's father, now dead, had left him at age two and had moved to California, never to contact him again. Dominic was the one to find his father and initiate contact when he himself moved west as an adult. Later that day, Dominic suddenly remembered that it was his father who had given him the fig tree with detailed instructions about how to care for it — in the age-old Italian tradition.

This happened during the time that Dominic was in therapy working on his feelings about his father's abandonment of him. That same day Dominic read that the Bo tree under which the Buddha was enlightened was a fig tree.

Synchronicity appears when a symbol that has been personally meaningful suddenly proves — or acts in accord with — its significance:

Rose Ann and her fiancé chose a beautiful engagement ring for her. The large diamond symbolized the indestructible brightness of their love for each other and their commitment to a lifelong bond. On their wedding day, they confirmed this verbally. But sadly, things did not work out as they had hoped. Four years later, they were divorced. On the day the divorce was final, Rose Ann was walking from the home of her new boyfriend back to her apartment. She was on a sandy road near the beach, still wearing the ring. From the corner of her eye, she saw something bright fall to the ground. Rose Ann knew instantly it was the diamond. It had suddenly fallen from its setting and sunk deep into the thick fine sand. Rose Ann stopped and looked carefully for it. Though she searched for a long time, it was nowhere to be found.

Synchronicity is the essence of timing, that mysterious readiness that occurs to defy our hesitation or control. It is the moment that can become momentum:

Irene's husband left her for someone else seven years ago. During the time following the divorce, she refused all contact with him even though he had admitted his betrayal, lamented hurting her, and asked if they could at least be sociable. Her friends suggested the same thing. But Irene was still feeling injured and crushed deep within. She worked on this in therapy, but the release from it did not come. One day she was walking alone along the beach when suddenly, out of nowhere, she suddenly experienced her hurt drop away, and she instantaneously knew that something had let go and that the time for contact had come. Irene went straight home and wrote her ex-husband a letter, and now the former couple are friends. Irene never regretted remaining true to her own timing, no matter what people thought of her. No one could have made her move a day earlier; no one could have stopped her a moment after.

There is synchronicity in the way we find our destiny in life through people and events that reflect our deepest needs and wishes:

Mother Teresa was born in Albania. At age fifteen, she heard of women who worked among the poor as missionaries. She was filled with an ardent desire to do that work. At eighteen, never having seen a nun, she left home for Ireland and joined the Sisters of Loreto, missionaries to India. Soon Mother Teresa indeed found herself teaching in Calcutta, but the convent and school were behind a wall and she was not allowed to work in the slums where she really wanted to be. At age thirty-eight, she was released by special permission of the pope to fulfill her dream. She felt bitter loneliness as she worked alone as a teacher of the poor with no money, supplies, or sisterly support. One day, Mother Teresa saw a dying woman and stayed by her on the street. This expanded her sense of her mission and she began ministering to the sick and dying. One nun had joined her. Now there are thousand of nuns and lay people continuing her work. Her destiny in the world began as a wish and ended in a work that helped those with needs and mobilized those with resources. Just the meetings and events occurred to make it all happen as she, and the world, needed it to happen.

There is synchronicity in the way a physical disability and/or an emotional wound becomes the threshold to our mission in life or to the unfolding of our talents:

Helen Keller is a moving example of this. Her own hardships became precisely what it took for her to find her destiny of service to others. In the film *My Left Foot,* we saw another example, this time in the realm of writing. In our own lives we may have been abused in childhood and now ask how that has helped us become bolder within ourselves and more compassionate toward others. "Because I was neglected, I learned to be self-sufficient. Because I was left out, I am more conscious of including others now." Our wounds are often the openings into the best and most beautiful part of us. We all recall the cruel stepmother in fairy tales. That archetype is often a necessary element in a fairy tale so that the heroine or hero can become a person of character and power. Stories often begin with a wound or loss or injustice and end with heroic acts of restoration and gift-bestowing love: "It takes just such evil and painful things for the great emancipation to occur," Nietzsche says.

Synchronicity is at work when something occurs that substantiates a belief or philosophy of life. This is a touching story told by Jung of an event that fit and confirmed his spiritual perspective. Another synchronicity in this story is its affirmation of the power of love:

In Upper Egypt, near Aswan, I once looked into an ancient Egyptian tomb that had just been opened. Just behind the entrance door was a little basket made of reeds, containing the withered body of a newborn infant, wrapped in rags. Evidently the wife of one of the workmen had hastily laid the body of her dead child in the nobleman's tomb at the last moment. She must have hoped that when the great man entered the sun barge in order to rise anew, the little stowaway might share in his salvation, because it was in the holy precinct within reach of divine grace.

 PRACTICE

• Recall a story from your own life that shows instances of synchronicity. Tell it to someone if you feel comfortable doing so. Read your favorite tale above to someone you think might benefit from hearing it.

• All the above examples actually occurred. Notice how, in every one of them, an increase of consciousness led to an increase in love, wisdom, or healing. Synchronicity is never for us only but for the world through us. Examine each story above and notice how in every one of them, without exception, someone was given the opportunity to go beyond ego, to be wiser, or to love more. Do not let any story go by without finding one or more of these facets of it. Now look at your own experiences of synchronicity to find the very same thing. Synchronicity happens so that we can advance toward our destiny. Keep track of future examples in your own life and resolve not to stop at amazement at how synchronicity happens but to recognize it as directive encouragement on your path.

Interpreting Synchronicities

A series of:	*May mean:*
Losses	Let go
Opportunities	Take hold
Information	Take heed
Failures to locate information	You do not need to know
False accusations	Let go of the need to impress
Everything going wrong	Step back
Physical breakdowns	Pay attention to your stresses
Easy transitions	You are on track
Embarrassments	Deflate your ego
Same old problems	This is where your work is
Betrayals	Relocate your trust
Memories	Let yourself grieve
Lessons in giving	Let go of attachment

A disclaimer is appropriate here: a series of losses may also respond best to *effort* instead of letting go. In fact, every entry above may be reversed. There is no reliable chart (or pilot) when it comes to navigating the seas of change and synchronicity. It is your call.

Synchronicity's messages become louder as they are listened to — as more letters are more likely from a person who knows you are reading them and responding to them seriously. Psychic literacy is the ability to read these messages; spirituality is the choice to respond to them. How do the messages come to us?

Synchronicity, dreams, intuitions, projection, psychic phenomena and readings, inner guides, events beyond our control, visions, sudden spontaneous powers, déjà vu, religious or hypnotic trance, meditation or contemplation, impetus from art or beauty, active imagination.

Spiritual choices are those that hearken to and say yes to these messages. To say yes is to let the Self take precedence over ego. A spiritual choice has two main characteristics: it expresses unconditional, universal love, perennial wisdom, and healing power, and it emanates from an unconditional yes to the conditions of existence. It includes an awareness of and a trust in the friendliness of psyche and matter. Since the transcendent has entered the temporal, consciousness is indivisible. Material events and tangible realities declare the conditions of the cosmic unconscious.

A spiritual choice is one that honors inner rhythms that may not match conventional milestone choices: "There are waves by which a life is marked, a rounding off that has nothing to do with events," wrote Virginia Woolf in her journal. Awareness of our personal spiritual messages helps us ride the waves rather than be drowned by them (overincorporate stimuli from outside) or run from them (underincorporate outside stimuli). *What in me has been steadfast through all the vicissitudes of my life? That is what has nurtured me.*

Finally, spiritual choices find a resonance in nature. "Man walks through forests of physical things that are also spiritual things and they watch him affectionately," said Baudelaire. Plato adds: "The motions akin to the divine part of us are the orbits of the universe. Everyone may follow these, correcting those circuits in the brain that were deranged at birth. We need to learn the harmonies of the universe." To learn from nature makes sense since we are part of her, and children resemble their mother. To allow seasons of blooming and decay, to welcome changing conditions and patterns, to hibernate in some seasons and activate in others, to live and be ready to die: these are nature's lessons and lesions. To acknowledge their applicability to ourselves is to join in their celebratory cycles of renewal.

A forestry sign at Patrick's Point in Humboldt, California, strikes a chord here: "Relentlessly, wave swells roll in toward the shallows, rise high, break into foaming crests, and plunge onto the shore. Waves are born when winds create friction with the sea's surface and infuse it with energy. As waves near the shore, the rising slope of the bottom of the ocean forces them into crests, and then into breakers. Waves release enormous energy when they crash upon the shore. All life in the surf zone must be able either to hide or to hold on for dear life."

How can one know which messages are from the inner Self and which are merely fictions of the mind? First, true messages feel so strong and real, they could not be otherwise. One has a felt sense, an intuitive certainty that they are authentic. Secondly, authentic messages arrive along more than one avenue, e.g., not only in synchronicity but also in dreams and intuitions. Thirdly, a true message does not submit to the ego's attempts to dismiss it. Finally, authentic messages move us in the direction of love, wisdom, and healing. They are never aimed at the self-serving ends or the aggrandizing designs of the ego. In our use of astrology or other divination modalities, do we seek wisdom about our spiritual path or advice about which investment to choose? The oracle of Delphi was closed in the fourth century. It had fallen into misuse and had lost its numinous power. People were asking ego questions — how to have more — rather than how to go beyond desire to destiny. There was no room left for miraculous wisdom, and so it passed away without protest. Oracular wisdom may be demolished in me once my ego ambition crushes my spirit of loving intent.

PRACTICE

• Using the chart above (p. 77) for interpreting a series of synchronous events, find examples in your recent or past life that fit the entries. How have you responded to the messages? Do these practices while in nature, e.g., hiking, walking on the beach, sitting under a tree, lying under the stars, etc.

• Graceful exits have dignity. Here are some hints that help us know when it is time to go (from a job, relationship, role, etc.): I give much more than I receive. I do more and more and see the success of less and less. I feel that I am giving up something rather than giving and receiving something. My health is suffering because of the stress of staying. Even what I once liked doing — and can do well — is now flat, stale, and uncomfortable. I am no longer effective. My bliss and enthusiasm are gone. I no longer come up with creative ideas or even see alternatives. I have been doing too much for too long for too little appreciation. I work on changing things but nothing gets better. Things keep going wrong and never quite right themselves as I am left with my finger in the dike. The same ineffective pattern keeps repeating itself. Money or prestige has become my central or sole motivation for staying. I do not move on because I am afraid to risk a change. I have no assisting forces encouraging me to stay. Synchronicities and dreams do not support my staying, only my going.

Does this apply to me in my job, relationship, commitments? If it does, what is the program for change that I know exactly how to implement but am not implementing? Take one baby step in that direction and another next week. If you find it extremely difficult to mobilize on your own, consider asking for help from someone you trust or seeking therapy. Not all the work can be done alone, or else why is there a world?

In the prologue, we met the three graces within: the inner physician, psychologist, and priestly guide. Therapists assist the client's inner psychologist and inner guide in their luminous work. They help build confidence in the trustworthy light within a person and foster the skills to let it come through. A client has something working within that is as wise as Freud or Jung. Therapists can invite that interior resource out and then facilitate a person's own follow-up skills. When a therapist sits with a client, the therapist is not alone in a berth with a hapless stowaway. The therapist is on the upper deck (realm of the higher Self) with an unrecognized master navigator (inner psychologist and guide) and an untrained sailor afraid of the voyage ahead but ardently wanting it to happen. With all of these forces working together, the client builds confidence and learns the ropes of life. Then the rigging can be nimbly handled and the rich port reached.

There is a lake in every man's heart and he listens to its monotonous whisper year by year, more and more attentively, until, at last, he ungirds. —George Moore

Chapter Three

WHAT SYNCHRONICITY REVEALS

The Time It Takes

Life, to be perfect, must be possessed altogether: there must be no past which is gone, no present which is going, no future which is to come. It must be permanent, abiding, full, and without succession. Life which would be past is lost life; that which is to come would not be life possessed; and that which is passing, is life in decay. —Edward Leen

Synchronicity plays out its pattern across the boundaries of time, since time and timelessness are also two sides of a single coin in the realm of the Self. Linear time is the mind's way of not being overwhelmed by the simultaneity that is happening everywhere within and around us. Time is a concept by which we describe our experience of change and movement. Are we living exclusively in time-bound awareness or in unity consciousness in which time and eternity are one? We are carefully tied to nature and history but only occasionally get a glimpse of it: "There is a morrow which mere lapse of time can never make to dawn," says Thoreau.

Cyclic time was acknowledged and revered by the ancients. New Year, in early times, coincided with the expulsion of demons and purification of the universe. It was a repetition of the original creation, an abolition of history as linear. New birth included death and resurrection: eternal return. Death is necessary for life to happen and for the cycle to continue. The moon is a symbol of this cycle since it appears, waxes, wanes, disappears, and reappears.

As we saw earlier, events to the ancients were not irreversible and thus not historical in our sense. In cyclic time, everything begins over again at every moment. "No event is irreversible and no transformation is final.... The desire to refuse history [in favor of archetypes] testifies to man's thirst for the real and his terror of losing himself by being overwhelmed by the meaninglessness of profane existence," says Mircea Eliade in *The Myth of the Eternal Return.*

In ancient paleo-oriental religions, revelation happened in mythic time, before the beginning of the world, and then was repeated in an archetypal way. In monotheism, revelation happens at a specific time and place, e.g., Sinai. Events of revelation become precious since they are no longer repeatable but are happening once and for all in a historic moment or as coming with a future Messiah. In this view the world is saved once for all in time. In traditional Christianity, the accent has not been on regeneration of the world but of the individual (since religious experience and faith are necessary for personal salvation). In that perspective, time is real because it leads to redemption.

Joseph Campbell proposes that "true mysticism releases you from time and then returns you to it." This is the conception of time as *kairos,* which in Homeric Greek means: "a penetrable opening." Kairos was also personified as the god of lucky coincidence (serendipity). Aion was the god of time (originally a vital fluid in all beings). Aion refers to eternal time: the *nunc stans:* the timeless moment beyond the flux of change. Aion does not abolish time but enlivens it spiritually. Since this time cannot be distinguished from normal time, we are confronted with a combination of opposites, exactly the paradoxical precinct most appealing to the Self and most scary to the ego! In the unconscious Self that speaks to us in dreams and synchronicity, there is

no serial time: past first, then present, then future. All time is simultaneous and inseparable in an unboundedly timeless present.
This is beyond the conceptual limits of the rational, left-brain
mind for which time can only be a succession of past to present
to future. Synchronicity is freedom from such succession.

Here is an example that may clarify how it is possible to enter
this other sense of time. I saw a video-movie yesterday that you
are seeing today. In the middle of your watching it, I walk in and
I instantly recall the scene you are seeing. I know what will happen to the characters on the screen in this scene and in the rest of
the film. I know this without having to take time to think about
it. I know all the fates of all the characters and the plot too in
one moment. I do not have to wait to know as you do. You know
the present of the movie and the past (beginning part) of it. You
do not know the future (how it will end). You are watching in
serial time. This is how the rational ego experiences time. I am
watching in simultaneity, the way the Self can experience time.
You may intuit what will happen next in the movie. Intuition is
knowing simultaneously without the time it takes to reason something out. Intuition transcends the serial and separable boundaries
of cause/effect and knows something in one simultaneous instant.
It thus knows in an acausal way. Synchronicity is acausal and
this is precisely how it is capable of taking us beyond the limits
of time.

Past and future are opposites in the conscious rational mind
and cannot be united. In the Self, opposites are joined and the
limitations of serial time-bound knowing are suspended. Mys-
tics knew in this same time-liberated way. These two elements
are what make us refer to this synchronous way of knowing as
spiritual.

Our task, as always, is twofold, psychological and spiritual:
to fulfill the demands of clock time and to honor the unbound
rhythms of the Self. We work out our destiny in hours and days
and are escorted to it at special moments under the sky of timelessness. This distinction may help: we are consciously aware

of clock time here and now. Synchronous time is all time simultaneously. It transcends clock time and we rarely notice it.
Occasionally it is noticed, and that is synchronicity.

In the fifteenth century, a clock was seen as a model of the divine plan: creation and redemption. The clock was revered as a
religious phenomenon until the eighteenth century. Thereafter it
was considered only a machine. A clock is a mandala in the spiritual perspective. Time is Yang and space is Yin. Together, they
manifest the Tao: the harmonious law governing the universe, the
meaning behind appearances. Time is the means of actualizing the
Tao: we work in time for the timeless. This is so unlike the concept we were taught: God is outside time and creates it. Whatever
we say of God, we say of psyche: I am the timeless experiencer
of timely moments. I am in time and beyond it. I am eternity
manifested in time/space events. Involution completes evolution,
unfolding what was always there — or rather here — not just
spinning out something new from what is not here yet. This is
the same time-transcendent consciousness by which we experience
spirituality.

The Egyptian god Aker, whose name means "this moment,"
was represented by two lions sitting back to back. The sun was
shown over the point of their connection. The lions' names were
"Yesterday" and "Tomorrow." They are the synchronicity of
simultaneous time connected in the center of the present and including the past and future. They were the doorkeepers of the
underworld. In mythology, the conjunction of opposites is the
gate to the underworld. It was believed that the death and rebirth of the sun occurred at midnight: the transforming moment
happens in the dark — where dough rises. In medieval alchemy
the new moon was the time of the conjunction of opposites
and of new life. It all fits, as do time and the timely, time and
timelessness.

J. S. Carroll writes: "Time is more than a mere succession of
corporeal movements. It is a procession of the light and love of
eternity into the temporal life of man." So the heart of eternity is

in the hands of time! We cannot hold back the hands of time but we can be held by them as we stand at the crossroads of every coincidence and then take the path with heart. It all happens in time. "In time" is meant in three senses: in the course of our lifetime, at just the right moment, and in time with the beat of the music of the spheres. Which spheres? Those of the earth and the sky and "*such* harmony is in immortal souls."

•

In addition to time, *number* also partakes of synchronicity. Jung wrote: "Number is the most primitive element of order in the human mind." Number is the archetype of order made conscious. Mathematical order manifests the dynamics of the psyche. Number is a symbol of the order of the universe and the oneness of psyche and matter. "Our psyche may have a numerical structure of order that is validated by matter and psyche, both lattices of a numerical field," suggested Marie-Louise Von Franz. An example of this is in the fact that the Fibonacci number series corresponds to the laws of plant growth. For the Chinese, number is the bridge between the timeless and the timely: a principle of orderly number underlies psyche and matter. RNA and DNA (the bases of heredity) use a mathematical code that corresponds to the *I Ching* hexagrams!

> *Attired with stars, I shall forever sit,*
> *Triumphing over death and chance, and thee, O Time!*
> — John Milton

The Knack of Knowing the Timing

Things take time. Impatience is a refusal to honor timing. Resistance in this context is being unwilling to go with the tide or being unready for it: "I have many more things to say to you but they would be too much for you now" (John 6:12). The readiness referred to here is timing. Timing is respect for the necessary incubation period that most transitions and changes require. The ego is not in control of it. It has a life and a clock of its own. "The revelation knows its own time and will only appear when it cannot possibly be mistaken for anything else," says Bernadette Roberts. Every feeling has its own timing. Grief is the best example. Haste or delay are useless.

The psyche is a wise system that knows just when to open to the world and when to close off from it. It is calibrated to external events, and so synchronicities convene to support it in either direction. Both are legitimate; only the timing is crucial. Thus, our healthy ego stabilizes itself through interactions, crisis, conflicts, and any ongoing traffic in the world. These are the vehicles by which we animate ourselves in the opening direction. Introspective and meditation are the vehicles for the inward direction. The first keeps the ego permeable, and the second keeps it safely intact. What we call depression may be a gross — but only — way of closing when other healthier styles do not seem possible. In any case, depression is a constant in the normal ebb and flow of life, nothing to be ashamed of.

A fully human journey requires a visit to both sides of the river of timeliness (see the chart on the following page). The left is active; the right is receptive. Both sides have a gift dimension. Both are initiatory *and* consolatory. Yin and yang are indelible features of the human psyche. In every archetypal story, we see the hero exploring both shores of the river of experience. Our ego makes us fear or feel ashamed of visits to the right side. We trust only effort and activity. Is this because we have noticed that its noise-making drowns out our panic about the gap, the void that opens when there is nothing that can be done? Is this what makes us more at home with changing things than with accepting things?

There is a tide in the affairs of men which, taken at the flood, leads on to fortune, omitted, all the voyage of their lives is bound in shallows and in miseries.   —*Julius Caesar*

There is a time to:	And there is a time to:
Take hold or hold on	Let go
Fight	Pull back
Take on more cargo	Jettison valuable cargo
Hold a hand	Let go of a hand
Poke	Prompt
Do	Be
Jump to it	Sit with it
Act on logic	Act on faith
Go for it	Enter more fully
Wait for it	Make a graceful exit
Be involved	Be alone
Control	Allow
Pull weeds (yank)	Pick figs (gently tug)
Say it	Be silent
Plan	Be spontaneous
Knead the dough	Let it rise
Hit	Bunt
Know	Not know
Create	Imitate
Break rules	Follow rules
Transcend boundaries	Honor boundaries
Show male/Yang energy	Show female/Yin energy
Use the time	Allow some idling
Reconstitute, resurrect	Fall apart, disintegrate
Feel whole	Feel fragmented
Be melancholy with Saturn	Be bright-eyed with Mercury
Make a choice	Take a chance
Achieve by effort	Receive grace

 PRACTICE

• Using the list above, carefully examine your life in the past six months and write in events, choices, and activities that fit for each of the entries. Notice where the preponderance of your responses fall. What is happening in your life now? Are you visiting one side exclusively? How can you balance yourself so that you visit both sides? Are you holding on when it is time to let go? Are you hanging in when it is time for a graceful exit?

• No matter how suddenly something may come to pass, it brewed for a long time in silence before it frothed. Timing is a way of referring to the natural incubation period that all births require. To respect timing is to allow that period, that pause in our souls as new things come to bloom in us. Becoming more loving, wise, and healing is a rebirth of Self from the ashes of the ego. It is a gentle thing and it takes gentleness to allow it. It is the essence of self-respect. We are not forced by fear or desire into delay or haste. We respect the timing of the self and yet keep gondoliering with optimism and alacrity.

Look at the time it took for you to work through the important issues in your life, to find the solutions to the important questions, even to know the questions. Look at the time it took to meet the people who could teach you just what you needed to learn, especially in relationships. How are you respecting or dishonoring your timing now? Do you allow time to take its course while at the same time you take action in a timely way? Find an example and practice this blending of movement and pause. Classical ballet uses precisely that same alternating combination.

Here is the test of time in the making of important choices: having to want something for thirty days straight before you trust that you really want it. How would your life be different if you had slept on all your important decisions in that way? Can you commit yourself to such a plan today? Others have timing that may be quite different from yours and may frustrate you. You especially want those you love to move forward and be successful. You sometimes try to force them to move more rapidly than they choose to. Respect of others is shown in respecting their readiness or unreadiness. When someone seems ready and is choosing not to move ahead, it is not appropriate to force or push that person, but to grieve what you see as a waste. Gentle encouragement, giving information once, and then a "hands off" policy may work best. Can you apply this to any relationships in your life now?

Only One World

The difference between the cosmos and man is only one of degree not essence.... Nature expresses something which transcends it.   — Mircea Eliade

The most brilliant fact that synchronicity reveals is the oneness of the world and our inner selves. They are, in effect, two aspects of one actuality: one universe that is simultaneously external (out there) and internal (in here). John Muir said of nature: "When we try to pick out anything by itself, we find it is hitched to everything else in the universe." We have a non-local mind, a psyche without limitations. No inside/outside means no limitations. We live in a natural orbit that is likewise unlimited in its interconnectedness. Quantum theory in modern physics acknowledges and confirms this when it sees particles not as mass but as interconnections: the relatedness of things *are* things. How significant that St. Thomas Aquinas's simplest definition of spirituality is interconnectedness with all things!

The fully extended psyche includes the "external world." Jung says: "The psyche is not localized in space.... The psyche is not in us; we are in the psyche.... The Soul is mostly outside the body.... Psyche and body are not separate entities but one and the same life.... Ultimately, every individual life is the same as the eternal life of the species." There is something in us that transcends us. This is the same something that beckons to us from nature. It is the call of the wild to spiritual wholeness. The Self calls the ego through nature. The inner world of the ego and the outer world of nature are facets of the cosmic Self. The medieval alchemist, Sendivogius, commented: "The greater part of the soul lies outside the body." Our mind is not in our cranium any more than Dan Rather is in our television. The brain is only the most local region of mind. We see again how soul work is world work! "The soul *is* the universe!" wrote Meister Eckhart.

In medieval times, the phrase *unus mundus,* "one world," referred to the unity of matter and spirit ever communicating. Joseph Campbell beautifully sums up the implication: "The hero and his god . . . are the outside and inside of a single self-mirrored mystery, which is identical with the mystery of the manifest world." The psyche and the universe is a hologram: all of everything is in every part of it all. Every cell of us is a hologram of the universe. All existence is a continuum of continuous creation that is still in rhythmic progress. The cosmos even found a way to become conscious to a high and mighty degree: *I am that way.*

Synchronicity is an affidavit that there is an *unus mundus,* a single reality with many locales. No dualism means opposites are relative, not independent. Nothing is mutually exclusive. Reality is not composed of wholes or parts but whole-parts. "The display (what we see) is dual but the reality is identical. . . . The reality of matter is the psychic self," says Mircea Eliade.

Marsilio Ficino, a Renaissance Florentine philosopher, saw the universe as one living being, with the cosmos as its body and the psyche as its soul. Synchronicity transcends and contains both psyche and matter, since synchronicities are sporadic moments in which the unity of psyche and matter becomes manifest. Every synchronicity is an epiphany of this unity. Every synchronicity is a death warrant to dualism.

David Bohm sees the universe as an indivisible whole and the observable world as an unfolded "explicate" order of an underlying enfolded "implicate" order. Both coexist hologrammatically (every part contains the whole). Matter and consciousness both have explicate (manifest) order and underlying implicate (hidden) order. "What is" is actually a psycho-physical unity behind which is a "vast sea of energy" which is unfolding in space and time. Synchronicity is also described in this same way, and so is everything about us.

Our body is not limited to the physical but extends in the universe — which is itself our larger body. Ecology is thus not about our taking care of nature as an object but as an extension of our own consciousness. Our body, physically, is one of the limited planes on which spiritual events can happen. Our body, hologrammatically, is not limited material but unlimited wholeness.

To be afraid of the ongoing tides of change is, in this context, not trusting the *unus mundus*, the oneness of the world of nature and our inner world. As we saw above, there is something about us that is independent of our personal story, i.e., something archetypal. The archetypes are psychoid: containing both psyche and matter. Nature is thus an assisting force in our destiny. Nature transforms death to life and continually promotes the union of opposites. This same synthesis happens in dreams and in synchronicity. In both, conscious and unconscious reveal our one life-affirming inclination toward Self-actualization. Desire gets in the way of our seeing this because desire is for something we believe we need outside, hence confirming our illusion of "out there." Synchronicity as a coincidence of outside events and inner processes confirms the unity of outside/inside and their passion to communicate. This is another confirmation that our dreams, ancient myths, and the perennial — archetypal — philosophy all say the same thing: "In the ever-present light of no boundary awareness, what we once imagined to be the isolated self in here turns out to be all of a piece with the cosmos out there," says Ken Wilber in *No Boundary*. Everything is synchronicity because everything is everything!

Claude Levi-Bruhl, the French anthropologist, originated a phrase to show the unconscious identification of humankind and the world: *participation mystique*. This fusion was symbolized by a totem (guardian) ancestral animal in primitive times. The belief in the one-with-all means that the ego has been deposed and materiality and spirit are aspects of the same unitary reality. Mircea Eliade writes: "In the most elementary hierophany, everything is declared. The manifestation of the sacred in a stone or tree is neither less mysterious nor less noble than its manifestation as a God. The process of sacralizing reality is the same; the forms taken...in man's religious consciousness differ."

The reality of the phenomenal world is an ongoing tide of transformation with which we learn to flow. A fixation on Apollonian order creates an obstacle to this Dionysian realization with its surprising challenges. For the ancient Greeks, the world would not survive if the Eleusinian mysteries (death/resurrection rites) were not enacted. This is a way of saying that our individual work and cosmic work are interdependent and one. It is the unity of Self and World that was covered up by the ego's pomp and circumstance, proclaiming itself as all there is. Recovered unity is thus what is really meant by higher consciousness.

The Self is two realities at once: an inner intimate identity and a mirror of nature/spirit: "You have within yourself the herds of cattle, flocks of sheep, and the fowls of the air. You are a world in miniature with a sun, a moon, and many stars," says a sermon of Origen. Nature is a theophany, an epiphany of the divine, and we are part of nature, not its opponent. The balance of nature is itself synchronicity. There is even another and more profound level of synchronicity in nature: its particular beauty on this planet is the only level of beauty that can satisfy such sophisticated humans as ourselves. Only this quality of nature can match the aesthetic sense that we possess.

An animal is equipped with a whole range of behaviors apposite to its environment. When a stimulus is presented, an innate automatic mechanism swings into action and an appropriate response is released. The animal acts in the best interest of its (and all of nature's) survival. In the same way, we inherit archetypal predispositions that endow us with all we need to flourish in our physical, emotional, and spiritual environment. They are like adaptive equipment in our psyche to help us respond to events and conditions of life in a spiritual, i.e., destiny-oriented way.

It is astonishing to realize that the equipment of nature and of the psyche are the same. They are homeostasis, self-healing, self-control, regulated growth, cyclic renewal. They are all geared to balance in nature's ecology and in our psyche. Here is an example of the similarity: the human body protects itself from overeating by feeling fullness after eating sufficiently. The psyche has a way of doing this too: compensation in dreams. A dream presents an image or a theme that shows us where we are becoming one-sided, top-heavy, in daily life. This is the transcendent function of the psyche in which a healing image cuts through and speaks truth to the ego.

It now seems clear that synchronicity is the meeting point of two realms: matter and psyche. In it the world archetype is united to the Self archetype. Synchronicity is the symbol and manifestation of the ultimate oneness of the inner world of the psyche and the outer world of matter. It is the parapsychological equivalent of the *unus mundus* — as a mandala is the inner psychic equivalent of the *unus mundus*. In both of these the psychic and the physical are one (essential) coin with two (existential) sides. One value results and distinctions disappear.

 ## PRACTICE

Contemplate the following quotations; restate them in your own words, and declare them to be already true of you:

We know the immensities of space better than we know our own depths, where, even though we do not understand it, we can listen directly to the throb of creation.   —Carl Jung

The true abyss is the human soul, . . . the terrifying immensity of the heavens is an external reflection of our own immensity. . . . In sublime inner astronomy of the heart . . . we see the Milky Way in our souls.   —Leon Bloy

There is no other I than the entire universe.... The center of myself is also the center of all creation and every single center is likewise a center of all creation.   —Deepak Chopra

Maybe saving a forest starts with preserving some of the feelings inside us every day.... If we cannot respect that interior land, neither can we respect the land we walk.
—David Lynch, *Twin Peaks*

I am he who is free and divine.... Many forms do I assume. ...And when the sun and moon have disappeared, I will still float and swim with slow movements on the boundless expanse of the waters.... I bring forth the universe from my essence and *I abide in the cycle of time that dissolves it.*
—Hindu Myth of Markandeya, *Marsya Purana*

All things are in sympathy.   —Hippocrates

My Dog Story

A dog is a perfect symbol of the meeting place of humankind and nature. All my life I have felt uneasy around dogs. I feared them. I abhorred their body odor, their jumping up on me, and especially their shaking water off themselves onto me. I then had occasion to be around Geezer, a good dog who, name and all, reminded me a lot of myself! One night in 1994, I saw a news clip on TV about wolves as the ancestors of dogs. This started an automatic chain of reflections in me. I did not try to think anything out, but allusions and images of prehistoric times kept coming to my mind unbidden. They soon captivated my imagination.

In an inner vision, I saw a cave clan huddling around a fire, eating and grunting in whatever monosyllables they could conjure. On the crest of a hill behind them was a wolf. He was watching them with great interest and with no intention of attacking. As he stared quizzically at the people and the fire in the dank night, he felt somehow drawn to them without chancing to approach.

One of the younger men noticed him in the moonlight and shadows. He, like all his fellows, was used to being observed by animals. He felt no fear, but he also noticed that he could not totally look away. His curiosity was sparked, and he felt a strange kinship too.

Night after night, the same scene replayed between wolf and man. One evening, with no prior plan, the man threw a piece of meat toward the hill. He was sharing the tribe's kill with the wolf. He noticed later, while the others slept, that the wolf gingerly crept down, snatched the meat, and ran off with it. Each night thereafter, this same scenario was played out, each time with braver, closer steps by wolf and man.

Now comes the quantum moment in the history of the relationship of man and animal. It somehow dawned on the man that the wolf could become an associate, a useful *friend*. Animals had always been enemies. This was a whole new concept, frightening and yet appealing! The combination of opposites — wildness and tameness — must have stunned and taxed the mind of this early valiant human. Within months, a wolf was almost a pet; within years a wolf was a dog.

In the theater of my imagination, I was struck strongly by one last feature in the story. I could see the wolf gazing and considering. I could see him wondering: "Can I trust this creature, man?" I could see him deciding: "Yes, I will trust him without yet knowing quite securely if I can." It was the moment of unconditionality, the moment when he threw his lot in with humankind, for better or worse.

The first wolf risk-taker initiated centuries of willingness to attach his fate to that of human beings. This decision instigated ages of love and abuse, pleasure and pain, generosity and rejection. That wolf decided to stay with us humans, to love us unconditionally, to seek us out, *to be happy only with us*. I could not get this one fact out of my mind. Something in that decision touched me profoundly.

I began to see dogs in a new way. I became more appreciative, more welcoming. The smell stopped bothering me, and so did the other qualities. All I could think of was how dogs need human closeness to be fully themselves. That realization led me to see dogs with compassion and respect. They do not fear human closeness, as I often do. They do not abandon their friends, as I sometimes have. They do not give up on the possibility of human kindness, as I might someday do.

I let go of my lifelong bias and fear. But more had happened, something more life-affecting and deeply crucial to my personal growth. I had grown in my comprehension of what love entails and how it sometimes smells not so good, or gets too wet, or knocks me down, or chases me, or dogs me, or wants to go out when I do not, or even wants to love me no matter how I smell or stay with me in any hell where I may dwell.

As he watched Adam and Eve being expelled from Eden, the first wolf/dog must have looked long and hard at his choice: the *sure* delights of the garden or the *chance* at happiness with the refugees. At the very last moment, before the gates slammed shut, he scampered out to join them and — as Milton reports in the final lines of *Paradise Lost* —

"In either hand the hastening angel caught
Our lingering parents and to the eastern gate
Led them direct and down the hill as fast...
They looking back, all the eastern side beheld
Of Paradise, so late their happy seat...
Some natural tears they dropped, but wiped them soon;
The world was all before them. . . . " and their dog beside them.

This story of mine is another example of how synchronicity can be extended in time. It does not always happen in a single moment. It can involve a long unfolding — like our hearts.

Is It Fate or Destiny?

*We are dragged along by fate to that which we refuse to
walk toward upright.*
                                                    —Carl Jung

The culmination of synchronicity is its direct revelation of destiny:
the design of the whole universe works itself out in the display
of each unique human life. "Life is a struggle to succeed in being in fact what we are in design.... Our will is free to realize
or not to realize the vital design we are but which we cannot
change or abbreviate" wrote José Ortega y Gasset. Jung adds:
"Free will is the ability to do gladly that which I must do." What
we refuse to bring into consciousness comes back to us as fate. It
hits us from without when we refuse to heed its summons from
within. It makes spiritual sense to forge a lasting agreement with
the universe, which can only be an unconditional yes to what
is. Attention to synchronicity helps us join unfolding processes
consciously. The word "design" adds the element of artistry.

Each generation presents to the universe a population of people
who have just the right ingredients in them to make the world better. Each person is a crucial cell in this mystical body of humanity.
Goethe wrote: "My work is that of a collective being and it bears
Goethe's name." Our work on ourselves makes us healthy enough
to transcend our immediate gratifications long enough to make a
contribution to the world. This is why compassion is always an
essential element of spirituality. "Individuation does not shut out
the world but gathers it to oneself," says Jung.

There is synchronicity in the fact that here and now the world
always has just the human resources that it needs to further its
evolution as is fitting for this epoch. Nature participates in the
same synchronicity by its drifts of species and seasons of growth
and change in each era. It creates an ice age and a temperate
age in accord with the overall requirements of evolution. I am
here at the right time — and just in time — for me to make my
contribution, and nature is supporting me by presenting just the

conditions that promote this enterprise. And so are all the people in my life.

Fate often allows a future to take shape regardless of our craft or plan or readiness. The ancient Greeks used a personification for fate: the three spinning sisters who decided on the length of each person's thread of life, love, and power. Lachesis controlled the length of the thread, Clotho spun the thread, and Atrophos cut the thread when the time for ending had come. This is a metaphor for the presence of a force or power that disposes what the ego proposes. Each enterprise, lifetime, relationship, power bond, consolation, grief has its own life span. There is a sense of something "greater than" myself that is at work beyond my control. This plan is my fate when I am at its mercy, i.e., caught off guard, fighting tooth and nail, shaking my fist at heaven. It is my destiny when I join in with it with ease, courtesy, and cooperation — although there is no harm in trying to massage and cajole the fates for a some extra time too! Synchronicity is what shows me where the thread is leading, how long it is, and who in my life is spinning it at the moment.

Destiny is often connected to career. Our work in the world is often our form of service or of actualizing our potential. Jonah is the biblical archetype of refusing one's destiny. Since he was needed as a prophet, his refusal of the call to become one was disregarded. He was swallowed by a whale and forced to swallow his pride. There are also times in the course of life when refusals are allowed to stand and then "a great prince in prison lies," as Donne says.

Jung said: "We find our destiny on the path we take to avoid it." The greatest of human tragedies is to be distracted from our destiny and to lose our power to activate our potential because of years of addiction to drugs, to alcohol, or to relationships that are abusive, unworkable, or depleting. A great potential in us can thereby fade away, and no one will do anything to halt the dissolution. The world will stand by as we throw away our fortune. We will stand by as we throw ourselves away. There is no guarantee that a whale will intervene for us as it did for Jonah or a tornado as it did for Dorothy. The challenge is to find our destiny in exactly what we are refusing to engage in. This is no easy task. It is hard to stop and look while we are running the other way! *Is my destiny scribbled on parchment, twirled in a bottle and hurled into the sea, to be stumbled upon only long after I am gone?*

Some people may find great success and seem to hit the target of their destiny in a career, and all the while they wish it were otherwise. In the film *Mr. Holland's Opus,* the main character was a great teacher who helped many young people achieve their potential. Mr. Holland was a born teacher, but he really wanted to direct a symphony orchestra.

We find ourselves not in charge of how it will be for us or in charge of how it has been. We realize that our wishes or even our choices or successes may give us no information about our real destiny. It is a mystery of synchronicity that life/destiny works just right for some and not for others. Synchronicity has a power beyond the ego's will, another way of saying that it is a grace with a will of its own.

The question arises: how am I responsible if things happen to me beyond my control? There is a seemingly contradictory answer to this in the *Iliad:* Agamemnon incites the wrath of Achilles by taking his woman slave from him. Agamemnon later says to Achilles: "Since destiny did this to me, I will give compensation." "What happened was incited by Zeus," adds Achilles. But the responsibility for amends is nonetheless Agamemnon's. We may not produce the "what is," but we are accountable for how we handle it.

There is no conflict in an enlightened person between law and freedom, since there is always a coincidence of personal will and that of the universe: the unconditional yes. By that yes, I am the embodiment of nature's laws and harmonies: each individual has the whole universe as his or her cause and effect, so personal meaning can be found only in our relation to the whole. Shakespeare states this so profoundly, as we saw above, in the speech we keep returning to from *The Merchant of Venice:* "Soft stillness and the night become the touches of sweet harmony.... Such harmony is in immortal souls."

> *No one knows what he has come into this world to do,...*
> *what his real name is, his enduring name in the register of*
> *Light.... History is an immense liturgical text where the dots*
> *and dashes are worth as much as the chapters and verses,*
> *but the importance of each is indeterminable and profoundly*
> *hidden.* —Leon Bloy

 ## PRACTICE

Destiny in Latin means to *determine*. It is used in the following senses: to set the time and place for a battle, to resolve to do something, to set the time for an execution, to ordain someone to an office, to aim a weapon, to betroth as a wife, to fix one's sights on something worth buying, to act intentionally. The definitions are all deliberate and conscious, denoting destiny not as something forced upon us but as something consciously sought. Look over your life story and notice three ways destiny seemed to happen to you and three ways in which you had a hand in it. Look more carefully and find a similarity in all six.

P.S. At this point, you may notice synchronicities happening more frequently in your daily life. Reading this book and being on the lookout for them can attract them to you.

A Fateful Story

This is an expansion on a story, probably apocryphal, full of synchronicities, about a medieval Catholic saint:

Julian, a haughty young nobleman, was out hunting one day when he was suddenly confronted, deep in the forest, by a mysterious white stag. Julian was startled and frankly bewildered when the stag began to speak. "You will not slay me but someday you will slay your parents." Profoundly troubled, and not ever wanting such a fate to befall him, Julian rode off secretly that very night. He found himself in another kingdom shortly thereafter. His skill with weapons soon distinguished him to all and, before long, he was invited to join the king's personal guard.

The king could not help but recognize Julian's prowess in battle, his integrity, his noble bearing, and even the strange poignant sadness that occasionally became visible in his face and made him seem more mature than his young years betokened. The king knighted Julian and thereafter gave him a castle and even his daughter's hand in marriage. Princess Catherine was beautiful and known for her piety and kindness to the poor. On their wedding night, Catherine inquired of her husband about his origins. Julian honestly confided to her about the prophecy and his self-imposed exile. She felt compassion for him for his superstition and fear and hoped that he would learn to trust God more.

Meanwhile, over these past two years, Julian's parents, grief-stricken and baffled by his departure, had gone searching for him far and wide. One night, while Julian was out hunting with his men, his parents, wearied with that day's travels, found themselves at his castle, unaware that it was the residence of their son. Princess Catherine greeted the strangers and invited them in. She was always kind to wayfarers and pilgrims who came to her door. As they sat together drinking ale by the fire, the old folks told the princess of their long search. As Catherine listened, she realized that these were indeed her husband's parents. What a wonderful surprise it would be for them to be greeted by Julian on the morrow! Telling them nothing yet, she gave them her own bridal bed and went to the chapel to offer thanks.

That same night, while camping in the woods, Julian overheard two of his men whispering about his wife. Not recognizing the falsity of their statement that she was unfaithful and kept a lover, he saddled his horse and rode at breakneck speed to the castle, his insulted and inflated ego ready to pop! Arriving before dawn — his wife still in the chapel — Julian ran breathlessly to the bedroom and indeed saw the outlines of two figures under the silken quilt. He despatched them both with sudden and spiteful blows of his sword as he screamed in rage and indignation. This brought Catherine from the chapel with a torch revealing the shameful bloody fulfillment of the stag's somber prediction. Julian and Catherine grieved together, and as a penance, turned their castle into a hospital for the poor. Lame and diseased came from far and wide to partake of their loving hospitality. Many found healing at the hands of their humble and ingenuous host who today is Saint Julian, the patron of hotel-keepers.

The Synchronous Embrace of Effort and Grace

The self cannot be gained by the Vedas, nor by understanding, nor by learning. He whom the self chooses, by him the self is gained. Nor is that self to be gained by one who is destitute of strength or without earnestness or right meditation. . . . The wise, having reached him who is present everywhere, enter him wholly. —Upanishads

There is nothing to be attained, yet I engage in action.
—Bhagavad Gita III

Our psychological work requires effort: handling fear, practicing assertiveness, dealing with inner child issues, addressing, processing, and resolving concerns in relationships. Our spiritual practice requires effort: meditation, mindfulness, rituals, prayer, compassionate action. As we saw above, these are the equivalent of kneading dough. But for bread to result, there has to be a period of rising, in which work ceases and nature takes over. This is the equivalent of grace: a force that takes over where will, effort, and intelligence leave off.*

---

*My book *How to Be an Adult: A Handbook on Psychological and Spiritual Integration*

Both effort and grace are necessary for integration — as both psychological work and spiritual practice are necessary for wholeness. Effort is a choice; grace is a free gift, beyond our control or skill of prediction. It cannot be conjured up by our effort. What we do simply places us in an apt position for grace to occur. Ultimately, however, effort may not yield transformation, and grace may come our way with no effort at all. The muses are personifications of grace. Any writer knows that the muse cannot be seduced by effort nor does she grant it. Pindar refers to this mystery when he says: "If happiness is possible to us humans, it requires struggle. Yet a god may bring it to us even now." Here is a model of what we have seen so far:

EGO: *conscious, existential*	SELF: *unconscious, essential*
Works personally by effort toward the goal of functioning optimally in relationships, in a career, and within oneself	Works spiritually by grace toward a destiny: to release its riches of love, wisdom, and healing into the world
Result: higher self-esteem and effectiveness through change	Result: consciousness and enlightenment through transformation
Told in one's personal story	Told in myth and metaphor
Presents challenges to make things happen	Asks only cooperation with what wants to happen
Cause leads to effect	Synchronous simultaneity
All based on steps we take	All based on shifts that happen

Grace is the advocate archetype, the assisting force that helps the hero when he has nothing going for him but his limited ego. It is often symbolized as the aid of a god or an elixir, talisman, or form of magic. Grace is that which cannot be willed by ego; it is a free gift of the universe/God/Higher Power. In Alcoholics Anonymous, recovery requires a spiritual program. Will power will not suffice. A Higher Power means the source of power beyond what ego is capable of, that which transcends the limits of

---

(Paulist Press, 1991), may be helpful in exploring these ideas and their implications in the context of the heroic journey motif.

intellect and will. We may instruct ourselves in knowledge (intellect) but wisdom is a gift. We may progress in spiritual practice but enlightenment is a gift. The attitude for work is gird your loins; the attitude for grace is surrender.

Grace means that the best things happen not because of what we do but because of what we are. As we are, we are already fitting vehicles for the light, thanks to the action of grace. Self-acceptance is an opening to this grace. Our ego will never yield only to effort. It takes a grace to surrender it. This is the concept of the twelve steps in Alcoholics Anonymous. "I am powerless" is admission that my ego is powerless. "Higher Power that can restore me to sanity" is the grace that picks up where control leaves off.

Every one of us is like Pinocchio. We were not born real; it is something we have to achieve and receive. At first we think it means: be normal: "Go to school and follow your conscience." Soon we find it is more than that. We have to confront our worst sides: see how we lie, how we look for a quick fix, how we still believe our addictions can content us in ice cream land. Then we see how we have to go into the belly of the dark whale (the shadow in the depths of unconscious) and be inventive enough to light a fire to help others live. Only then are we reborn from the dark, i.e., spit out of the whale's mouth. Then and only then are we ready to become real, but we are still not real yet. We cannot do the last part ourselves. The Blue Fairy has to lean lovingly over the body of the broken boy. We are blessed if we arrive at that moment: a disassembled, dissolved ego ready for rebirth. The Blue Fairy (feminine intervention) represents the grace that makes us whole. Effort (masculine power) was not enough, not even heroic effort. It takes the wand of grace to tap us. Then the process is complete. The reality of liberation is achieved *and* received.

Before the work, before the journey, we are still only makeshift persons, headpieces filled with straw, only parts held together with ego mucilage. We are all wooden heads until we achieve a crossing of the thresholds and all along the path receive the grace we need. Achievement may only congratulate and inflate the ego; grace completes it. Spiritual materialism means enlightenment will happen by effort. Spiritual sanity and spiritual adulthood see past the omnipotent displays of ego.

An essential feature of grace is timing, synchronicity. The chick cannot break out of its shell until its beak is firm enough to crack it. Only then will its effort in pecking at the shell yield liberation from it. The timing is graceful and synchronous: the food supply in the egg ends at precisely the time the chick is ready to emerge. This is also a metaphor for the work we achieve and the grace we receive to make our work effective.

Timing also means pacing. Babies pace their birth unless they are rushed through it, in which case they suffer a birth trauma because they cannot *track* their experience. Our respect for our own timing makes it possible for us to track ourselves and process our life events. This is how we become conscious and gain a sense of personal power.

Joseph Campbell says: "The images of myth are reflections of the spiritual potentialities of every one of us. Through contemplating these, we evoke their powers in our lives." As an example, we have the theme of the sword in the stone, i.e., Excalibur, which tells us that spiritual power is hidden in the dark and can be released with ease if it is our destiny to release it. The special capacity comes only to the one who fits *this* story: only Arthur can free Excalibur, not knights from other ancestries or Prince Charmings from other stories.

Grace often enters the hero story at the moment when the hero has the clearest sense of his inadequacy. This is the dismemberment theme: we find ourselves in pieces. A force comes to us that takes us beyond our own limits and enlarges us, i.e., makes us whole. A hero story seems to require constant action, but within the struggle phase there is always a period of captivity, a pause that allows other forces to come into play. Robin Hood takes action, but then he is in chains until Maid Marian helps him. Even the dungeon, i.e., the void, is part of the path. *We think back on all our wasted, unconscious years. Were they the rising of the dough, the necessary darkness? Were they the necessary pause like the one before the finale of fireworks? This is an apt metaphor, since what is a pause to us watching from afar is a busy time to the pyrotechnician whose operations we do not see.*

Another threshold of grace is in the hero's inability to perform the task at hand. This is a metaphor of how the psyche is sometimes unconscious of its powers. An example is the miller's daughter unable to turn straw to gold in *Rumplestiltskin* or Psyche's inability to sort the grains of Aphrodite. The ego is unable because the Self is unready or asleep. Grace is the awakening of hidden powers. A legitimate part of the heroic struggle is containment. Sometimes the task is to hide or sleep. The ego's work is simply to sit or be taken blindfolded or be under spell. Examples are Jack in the cupboard of the giant's wife, Snow White in her casket, Christ in his tomb, Dorothy asleep among the poppies, Joseph in prison. This is not wasted time, but the simmering necessary for the soup to be ready. It is the dough rising. It is like dreaming in which psychological and spiritual work are being done while we remain unconscious.

We fear a visit to the far side of the ego, where control dissolves and action is ineffective. Quiet gaps seem ominous, boring, or lacking in the adrenaline rush we are accustomed to. We fear having no story. Yet marvels happen best in the pause between plot developments. This pause is serene attentiveness: "Be still and know." Yet we also hear a summons to activate ourselves: "Be swift my soul...be jubilant my feet!" These recommendations seem contradictory, but only to the intellect. In the psyche's world they deftly combine apparently opposing but truly legitimate phases of our work. The result of such a combination happening in us is the inner rainbow, i.e., the full spectrum of the light.

The key to our deepest happiness lies in changing our vision of where to find it.   —Sharon Salzberg, *Lovingkindness*

PRACTICE: Mindfulness

The "pause between" effort and grace is mindfulness: the conjunction of a step we take and a shift that happens. It is a practice to begin today and continue as a part of your daily routine: Sit comfortably with eyes closed and with your cupped hands in your lap, paying attention to your breathing. Notice your breathing in, breathing out, and the little gap between the breaths. That momentary stillness is the spaciousness of no-mind, freedom from the ego's storylines of fear and attachment. Rest in it! If thoughts interrupt, simply label them as thoughts and return to awareness of your breathing. Form an image of your present crisis, problem, or concern and imagine that you are holding it in your hands in the form of a ball. Notice whether you chose the image of a baseball, tennis ball, etc. Acknowledge it as yours. Notice how heavily it weighs and let your hands drop farther down if appropriate. Now imagine that the ball is covered with five layers, each of which you will examine and then shed.

The first layer is that of fear: what is scary about this problem and how are you holding on to the fear or being stopped or pushed by it? Once you are aware of your felt sense of this fear, imagine that you are peeling it away from your problem ball and dropping it aside. You affirm: "I let go of the need to fear this."

The second layer is that of control: how invested are you in controlling the outcome of this problem and how are you trying to maintain control of others around you? Once you are aware of your felt sense of this need to control, imagine that you are peeling it away from your problem ball and dropping it aside. You affirm: "I let go of the need to control this."

The third layer is that of blame: how are you blaming this problem on someone else? Once you are aware of your felt sense of this blaming, imagine that you are peeling it away from your problem ball and dropping it aside. You affirm: "I let go of the need to blame anyone for this."

The fourth layer is that of shame: how are you feeling shame and guilt about having this problem? Once you are aware of your felt sense of this self-recrimination, imagine that you are peeling it away from your problem ball and dropping it aside. You affirm: "I let go of the need to feel ashamed of this."

The fifth layer is that of the need to fix the problem: how are you letting your serenity become dependent upon whether you can bring everything back to normal? Once you are aware of your felt sense of this burdensome task, imagine that you are peeling it away from your problem ball and dropping it aside. You affirm: "I let go of the need to fix this."

Return your attention to your breathing, noticing the gaps between the breaths as well as the breaths themselves. Notice if the ball feels lighter. (Has it become a ping-pong ball?) Ask yourself what is left of it. Can it now be pure space, like the gap between your breaths? Now touch the earth with your cupped hands and lift them over the crown of your head as you open them and let go of what is left of the problem in a gesture of offering and releasing. Open your eyes and give thanks to the first thing you see in nature. *Support from nature was the experience of grace for Buddha, who touched the earth as his witness and who gazed with thanks at the Bo tree for seven days in thanksgiving for being enlightened under it.*

You are now the fair and alert witness within and outside your problem. Something has been born that sits safely in the center of and yet also beyond the entanglements of the struggle. Free of dualisms, neither stoic nor stuck, you can observe conflict with feeling and yet with focus on its meaning and challenge. This is attention to both the figure and the ground of whatever faces you. Nothing really has to be complicated or confused. The embroideries of ego create those conditions. You can locate the simplicity and — unbearable? — lightness of your being through mindfulness. You can freely go with the flow of your life and, *at the same time,* be able to hearken back to a reliable stillpoint that is impervious to the ups and downs of your drama. This stillpoint *is* oneness: the ultimate spaciousness behind all the appearances of things and behind all the layerings of ego. The stillness may last only for a moment but it is delicious enough to keep you coming back for more and it is only a breath away. *Any issue granted this kind of egoless attention becomes a silence richer than words and always leads to surprises.*

We have an inner inclination — even an urgency — to be open to what is and to attune to reality as it is. The human-made mind wants to dress up reality in accord with its own fears and desires. These are attempts to protect our opening self from hurt and disappointment. Such attempts prove the existence of our vulnerability. We do not have to doubt that we know how to open. We do not have to try to open; we are always and already at it. The work is to catch ourselves at closing. This is what mindfulness achieves. Ken Jones writes: "Mindfulness is a practice of attentive yielding and accepting of the body and emotions, which gradually dissolves our futile root habit of conducting an emotional lawsuit with everything that balks or threatens us."

"No Room for Chance in the Meaningful World of the Psyche"

Chance is the unpredictable, unexpected, and unknown element in events that surprises us happily or unhappily. It has no explanatory cause. It is a random event in that there is no recognizable pattern or plan behind it. Yet Heinz Kohut was perhaps referring to something that transcends chance when he spoke of "the healing power of the random array." Synchronicity takes chance occurrences and relates them to our destiny by their meaningfulness. This is how synchronicity goes for higher stakes than chance or luck.

Chance or luck is mere coincidence, i.e., synchronization. Synchronicity is meaningful, life-affecting, destiny-promoting, spiritually encouraging coincidence. Chance and synchronicity will look the same in their display of an event, but they are worlds apart (literally!). What makes chance into synchronicity is the consciousness in us of the vaster design that is unfolding. Chance happens to us; synchronicity happens in us. This is another way of seeing the crucial relationship between synchronicity and consciousness.

Within this distinction is the spiritually founded belief that more is going on than meets the eye, that behind the appearance of randomness is an order and that this order wants to manifest itself. This belief does not necessarily entail theism. One can lay aside the traditional concept of a personal God and still believe in an implicit order in the universe that works itself out in each of us in unique ways. This orderly calibration of the universe has as its goal the harmony of humankind and nature, person and person, matter and spirit. *Something, we know not what, is acting we know not how, in every heart, and we do know why: to release into the existential world the essential reality of love, wisdom, and healing.* The Tao expresses it this way: there is something formless yet complete that existed before heaven and earth. How still! How empty! Dependent upon nothing, unchanging, all pervading, unfailing. . . . I call it meaning.

Actually, chance and order work together. A striking example of this is in the proportion of men and women in the world. There is not a major disparity — though there are more women. The gender of a fetus is based on chance, and yet some other force is at work that keeps the population reasonably equalized. The law of probabilities is at work in this, numbers reflecting and even fostering the order in the universe and its correlation with chance. The question of whether we choose our parents arises here and may be answered: it is not choice and not chance. Our inner scientist may not understand that paradox but it makes perfect sense to the Delphic priestess answering inside us!

Chance may simply be a playful way the universe has of collaborating with us in the working out of our destiny. Thus synchronicity integrates the irrational into an orderly pageant of evolution. The challenge is always the same: to believe in the artistic design in spite of the random display. The record shows us humans to be crassly ignorant and destructive but also touchingly responsive and restorative. Perhaps Gandhi expressed this tension between our existential display and our essential design most accurately: "I see that mankind still survives after all its attempts to destroy itself and so I surmise that it is the law of love that rules mankind."

> *Heaven from all creatures hides the Book of Fate,*
> *All but the page prescribed, their present state . . .*
> *O blindness to the future, kindly given,*
> *That each may fill the circle marked by heaven:*
> *Who sees with equal eye, as God of all,*
> *A hero perish and a sparrow fall,*
> *Atoms or systems into ruin hurled,*
> *And now a bubble burst and now a world.*
>
> — Alexander Pope, *Essay on Man*

Chapter Four

CONDITIONS
AND CRISES

The Givens of Human Life

The poppy petals:
How calmly
They fall.

—Etsujin

The conditions of our human existence can be embraced with acceptance or opposed with rebelliousness. A healthy person accepts the conditions when it is clear that they are irreversible. At the same time, that person also struggles to change a particular condition if it yields to such change. Grace provides the wisdom to know the difference.

The givens of life have been variously referred to as "Adam's curse," the will of God, or the human condition. They are universal in that no one is exempt from them or immune to them nor can any be repealed. We individuals are not victims of these conditions; they are simply the human reality. To contemplate this fact is to ask oneself: Am I willing to share the confusion and pain of my fellow human beings? Can I face life "not as a victim or a fanatic but as a seafarer who can greet with an equal eye the deep he is entering and the shore that he must leave" (E. M. Forster, *Howard's End).*

These are not just the conditions of existing; they are the conditions of evolving. They are the prerequisites for a human story to

113

Adult Response	GIVENS	Childish Reaction
I stay with myself.	*I am alone with no rescuer or rescuer.*	I fill the aloneness with externals.
I stay with the normal stages: rise, crest, decline, realign, let go.	*All is transitory, impermanent, and changing. Nothing satisfies forever.*	I fixate: holding on, addiction, clinging, control. Trying to hold back the hands of time.
I allow it all to unfold.	*Life is unpredictable.*	I seek safe harbors and certitudes.
I accept what cannot be changed; I attend to what can be changed.	*Suffering is part of life: both physical and emotional.*	I am entitled to immunity. I am exempt from the law of averages. I deserve special treatment.
I accept that things are not always fair.	*Things are not always fair.**	I believe that punishment of evil and reward of good will happen now or later.
I accept that some things are too big for me to handle.	*Sometimes we will be faced with more than we can handle.*	I will never have more to face than I can handle.

*If things were fair, we would hate it! We hate and fear death because it is fair.

unfold with character, purpose, and meaning. They make us the fascinating characters we are; they make our human story the intriguing plot that it is: Only alone do I find my unique path. Only in a transitory world do I transcend time for the timeless. Only in an unpredictable universe do I expend all the effort I can muster. Only in suffering do I make contact with my inner resources of strength. Only in a world of pain am I moved with compassion and do I act with love.

These givens are thus precisely what it takes for us to be and become who we are. Confounding realities, like aloneness, the suffering of the just, the pain required for growth, cease to be questions when our spirituality is founded on a stabilizing trust in the aptness of these conditions for evolution toward our destiny.

Such trust is the trusty horse on which we ride out the chaotic times in life. The conditions of existence are meant to be like weather conditions: if I live in a house with a sturdy roof, walls, and a foundation, I let the storms come and I abide: *Though the seas threaten, they are merciful...(The Tempest)*.

It is synchronicity that we have healthy responses in us to match the very conditions that we are confronted with. We have tears to process our grief and smiles to express our merriment. We have inner sources of nurturance to deal with loneliness, capacities for acceptance and for changing, and bodies capable of handling varying moods in ourselves and in others.

We may wish there were a savior who would release us from these harsh exigencies of our humanity. But any savior figure who has appeared has submitted to the conditions, not abrogated them. To paraphrase Elie Wiesel: "There is no messiah but there are messianic moments when we choose to care and to humanize our destiny." We are messiahs to ourselves and to the world when we say yes with gracefulness and gratefulness: "A man whom fortune's buffets or rewards hath taken with equal thanks!" (*Hamlet*). Shakespeare proposes thanks in the face of life's givens. Jung also proposes an etiquette when facing the conditions: embrace them with "an unconditional yes to that which is, without subjective protests, an acceptance of the conditions of existence...an acceptance of my own nature as I happen to be." Buddhism suggests one also: "joyful participation in the sorrows of the world." The Gita expresses it too: "...the same in suffering and joy, content always." St. Ignatius recommends that these tidal laws of our life be greeted with "holy indifference." He recommended equilibrium in the face of life's conditions not as stoic indifference but as detachment. Goethe has this suggestion: "As long as you have not grasped that you have to die to grow, you are a troubled guest on the dark earth." Mircea Eliade adds, in speaking of the hero: "The law of life lives in him with his unreserved consent."

Our modern myth, based on fear and denial of these givens, seeks to extinguish necessary decay by health fads and cosmetic interventions. Our movies repeal the condition of unfairness with happy endings in which good always triumphs over evil. We have enlisted the courts to compensate our every loss, even the ones *we* are accountable for. We thus use the law to indemnify our losses so that we will not have to grieve over them. We are fearing and avoiding the very feeling that gives us sensitivity and character. Have we forgotten that Demeter, goddess of life from earth, and Persephone, married to Death, are mother and daughter? They are metaphors for life and death united in one cyclic process. Have we lost sight of the myth of the wounded healer, the one who bears endings, grief, and calamity and thereby brings salvation? (Salvation means freedom from the fear and attachment of the ego.)

Our ego experiences life through the cycles of fear and craving instead of the cycles of letting go and going on. In fact, our lifelong attachment to the drama of fear and desire is what confirms the existence of ego. This is its appeal. Once we see this, we automatically change the way we live. We have exposed the way we relate to others and to life predicaments as part of an ego-reinforcing habit. Now that we have exposed it, we can more easily eliminate it. Attachment to drama is not wrong or sinful. It is an error, since nothing can be held on to in this transitory existence. It is mistaking excitement for pain.

Once we realize that all is impermanent, there is nothing to grasp or cling to or control and no one to do the clinging. If all things are impermanent, then so is the ego that desires them. "I let go my insistence on control and entitlement. I drop the need to uphold my ego. I stop using you to end my loneliness. I stop being so possessive in my relationship with you. I let go of seeing you as territory. I do this by giving up my defending of my ego territory in favor of the spacious territory of my vulnerable bond with you." This is how we renounce the premises of ego in the context of healthy relating.

There is an intriguing Zen response to the condition of impermanence. Two terms are used: *danken* (all is impermanent so accumulation is useless) and *joken* (maintaining our commitment to work toward goals of health and welfare anyway). Each of these alone is one-sided. To accept the combining of impermanence as a condition as well as the legitimacy of goal orientation is the Middle Way of Buddhism: "I endure and overcome with no attempt to resolve. I am defenseless against life's surprises and simultaneously resourceful in the face of them." This combination of defenselessness and resourcefulness is the foundation of freedom from fear. They are alternate words for yes.

A practice is to leave our roses in the vase long after they are withered. Learning to appreciate each phase of a flower's life — from bud to death — is a way of expanding our sense of impermanence to include the beauty of its seasons.

Religion is designed to respond to the givens of existence. Consolation comes from belief that the immediate existential experience is not the whole reality. In Christianity, for example, behind the appearance of aloneness is a promise of presence: "Behold, I am with you all days." Impermanence is addressed by St. Paul: "For when this earthly tent is folded up, there awaits us a tabernacle not made by hands." To the question of whether I will have to face more than I can bear, I hear: "My grace is sufficient for thee." To the problem of unpredictability comes the response: "Heaven and earth will pass away but my words will not pass away." To the suffering of the just: "Take up your cross and follow me.... You shall have reward in heaven." To the lack of fairness is the promise of final justice at the Last Judgment when God "will separate the sheep from the goats" for eternal reward and punishment. Religion can be used to shield us from the full brunt of life's conditions, promising repeal in this life or the next. Adults with faith might ask themselves if they seek the consolations of God or the God of all consolation who often does not console but allows people to face the givens baldly and boldly. Jesus on the cross, in his forsakenness, did just that. "In him there was only yes...."

One of the conditions of existence is that sometimes we will be faced with more than we can bear. There is a capacity in the human psyche to handle the conditions of its existence, just as animals have innate capacities and instincts to deal with theirs. *Our innate capacities can be developed as programs of skill* to deal with aloneness, unpredictability, unfairness, transitoriness, suffering, etc. This is the sense in which we can handle things — always one day at a time, of course.

Occasionally, the little rain that must fall into every life becomes a hurricane. A non-stop series of disasters occurs that lays us low or casts us into the void. This puts too much pressure on our capacity to handle things, since it is happening too fast for the "one day at a time" approach. There is no power that is seeing to it that this will not happen to *me*. One of the conditions of existence is that anything can happen to anyone. It is normal to break down under such pressure and then reconstitute later. Suicide is the rejection of this possibility.

In a breakdown, it is normal to have runaway feelings: anger may keep flaring up uncontrollably; sadness may lead to crying jags; fear may lead you to be phobic about almost everything and even superstitious and paranoid. Obsessive thoughts may plague you. All of these are normal when they are phase appropriate, i.e., characteristic of the first blush reaction to the overwhelming crisis. When you are basically functional, they end as you move toward acceptance and resolution. In a neurotic character structure, the inappropriate feelings, behaviors, and thoughts hang on indefinitely.

Nature's conditions can be handled. But the conditions placed by the ego, the human-made dramas we create to make our lives painful (even decorative and entertaining!), do not have corresponding programs with which to handle them. We are amateurs every time. For instance, you can handle a physical death of a partner but perhaps not the daily death in your abusive relationship. This is a condition devised by the ego and requires more help than an individual ego can muster. A support system is often a prerequisite.

Life is continually baffling us with its contradictions, and we can be overwhelmed and demoralized by them or we can allow them to pass through us with equipoise. *The unconditional yes that allows us to be defense-less releases our lively energy that makes us resource-full.* This combination of letting go and taking hold frees us from possession by the givens and renders us able to relate to them. The givens of human existence are not inconveniences to be put up with but the most appropriate and precise conditions for the achievement of our highest goal! They are *steps* we tread to transformation. They are a path, like synchronicity, to the release of unconditional love, wisdom, and the power to heal ourselves and others. They are also the conditions that beings like us require if we are ever to have depth. Without these blows and challenges, we would be empty Pollyannas in a superficial world.

The conditions of our existence are assisting forces on the path to our destiny: Without aloneness, I never would have found the vast inner world of wisdom and healing power within me. If what I see and desire were not transitory, I never would have looked beyond or through the persons and things in my life to contact the transcendent. If all were predictable, my eyes would never be opened by surprises, by the unexpected, by serendipity. The element of surprise in synchronicity is the Dionysian spirit, granting us access to a lively energy that transcends the limitations of orderly logic. Without suffering, I would never have found my inner resources, never have felt the grief that gives me depth and character, never have opened my heart to compassion. If things were always fair, I would have no motivation to recognize and handle the shadow in myself and others in creative ways.

 PRACTICE

• Taoism is a Chinese philosophical system that addresses the conditions of existences through respect for synchronicity. The Tao is the harmony of the universe, and to act in accord with it is happiness (as well as sanity). Tao makes reality the same as lawfulness. In the Hindu and

Buddhist traditions, dharma is the moral law that upholds the universe in an orderly way. These are ways of acknowledging the meaningful interconnectedness of all things. Our destiny is to make and carry through the decisions that support and synchronize with the reliable order of Tao and dharma — always and already in progress. Tao grants primacy to a force beyond the ego that does not impose order but exposes it. This is the synchronicity of time, people, and events that come to meet us and to show us our destiny. To honor the Tao is to commit ourselves to the unfolding story by cooperation with these co-operators. Since psyche and universe are one reality, the same Tao that works personally with us is also the invisible workings, the order of the world. Something in us is enthusiastically geared to harmonize with that order and rhythm. It is not a logical decision in our brain but a musical disposition in our soul. True work on ourselves flows from and with this rhythmic urge toward wholeness within and around us. Read *The Way of the Tao* by Lao Tzu as a manual for facing the givens of existence.

• The Roman poet Terence writes: "Nothing human is alien to me." To be human is to be susceptible to all the conditions of existence and not in control of any of them. Healthy people have made peace with that. We cannot have control, but we can have a program, a plan, a mechanics to deal with the things that happen to us. It is wise and necessary to have a ready resource to meet every human need in the course of life. Experiences and crises are meant to deepen us and to show us our path. When we have no program, we lose those options. We have safe passage but no threshold to cross. We survive but may fail to evolve.

Earthquakes show us how little in control we are. Yet there are earthquake safety rules we can follow. This is the program that gives some measure of control to our response so that we can get through it with the least amount of damage. It is fascinating to notice that the old advice on earthquake safety was to tense against it in a doorway. Now the recommendation is to go with the movement, to roll in the hallway, our bodies balled up to avoid too much impact. This is wisdom about how to combine control and surrender.

Here are some examples of programs to have in place when facing various predicaments. These are tools of the healthy ego! Each provides a way of *going on:*

• When I am afraid, I can admit my fear, allow myself to feel it fully, and then act as if the fear could not stop me.

• If I am angry, I can express it responsibly and directly to the person involved without blame or violence.

• If I am passive in my interactions with others, I can learn to be assertive and to stand my ground without becoming aggressive.

• When I suddenly feel fragmented and depressed because my life seems to have been a waste, I can imagine a kindly, avuncular voice inside that says: "It's not so bad as that. Look at all you have done. You made some mistakes, but everyone does. What matters is that you have gone on and know better now. Give yourself some credit!"

• In the void — the black hole of panic in which nothing works and our lively energy is on hold — we can simply stay in the suspense, without having to do anything. We can let it be and listen to its eerie silence until we feel an impetus to move in some new direction. The timing is never from ego (the real meaning of "not in control") but from the Self's world of synchronicity.

• If I feel guilty, I can make amends and resolve to change my behavior for the future.

• If someone says something cruel to me, I may be tempted to resort to the ego's program of retaliation. Instead, I can declare to the other how hurt I am to hear that and how it is unacceptable to me to be spoken to in that way. When the ego voice within says: "You should have come back at him with this...," you can acknowledge that as ego, and respond with an affirmation: "I let go of the need to retaliate. I choose to handle things creatively, strongly, and kindly." The work is to clear away all the ego's programs from our modus operandi and to replace them with loving and assertive ones.

- If I am deserted by a partner who has found someone else, I can resort to the ego's armory and defend myself against further hurts by putting up a wall against future relationships. Such self-defense walls me in. On that wall, the scared ego has scratched its self-defeating graffiti: "You cannot trust men [or women]. They will always betray you. You cannot handle the normal give and take of relationship with all its potential for pain. Stay away from all future relationships." I may believe these bitter verdicts and thus abandon myself. Suddenly, passion goes out of my life, as do my chances for pleasure and growth. It is stressful to maintain a repression of the natural human instinct to bond. Wholeness means giving free rein to all our instincts and susceptibilities. Healthy people are willing to love again, ready to risk the same disasters they faced before, because they have found a resource for future reference. Griefwork is the program for dealing with betrayal and abandonment. Those who have grieved and let go will choose new partners more wisely and be more psychologically nimble in their grieving the next parting, if that were to occur.

These are strategies to face the givens of our lives, not to escape them. None of these programs includes drugs, food, sex, or other compulsions. None of them resorts to silver lining consolations that are not true and that contradict the conditions of existence. Examples are: "Well, I always did my best." None of us has always done our best throughout our life, nor is that to be expected. "Things will always work out for the best." Things will not always work out for the best, as the Holocaust has shown. "It is karma." This is a deterministic use of the concept of karma that may serve to excuse us from adult responsibility for our actions. "God will provide." Provision for human needs will not always happen, as starving children learn each day. We have to provide for ourselves — and others — in many ways.

- Sometimes we face something that is too big for us to handle alone. Then our program is to seek help. If I have a cut on my finger, I can use the program of first aid that I have lined up for just such emergencies: peroxide and Band-Aids close at hand. If I cut an artery, I will have to go for help to the hospital where the doctor will provide the necessary program of suturing me. Likewise, in a psychological crisis, I may need to consult a therapist to help me design a program that meets my needs with a healthy resource. Becoming healthy does not mean that things no longer happen to us but that we now have ways of handling whatever may happen.

Here is a summary model for healthy functional responses to the conditions of existence. What can I install into my lifestyle to make these happen more and more?

Deal with:	*By:*
ALONENESS	Building a support system
TRANSITORINESS	Letting go
UNPREDICTABILITY	Trusting synchronicity
SUFFERING	Accepting what cannot be changed, changing what can be changed
UNFAIRNESS	Accepting what cannot be changed, changing what can be changed

Finally, we can admit that even the healthiest ego may be powerless to effect certain changes in the psyche. No psychological program works to make arrogance surrender easily; it cannot "turn the other cheek," love or forgive unconditionally, or give itself away in compassionate generosity. These are callings from a spiritual source that not everyone will hear. They hearken from the world of the Self where grace presides. How ironic — and humbling — that we cannot release what is best in us on our own!

• In quantum physics, the "Principle of Indeterminacy" refers to the fact that chance and unpredictability meet at the very heart of matter. Evolution brings order to this chaos, but the chaos remains nonetheless. Our personal work is to contain just such opposites within ourselves. This means allowing crises to unfold and doing all we can to evoke harmony from them. This is welcoming what enters our world and waving good-bye to what wants to go. Perfect joy happens in the world we no longer oppose. Answer these questions in your journal: What is chaotic in my life? How can I allow the chaos? How can I bring harmony and order to it? What is ready to be said good-bye to? What is ready to be welcomed? What am I holding out against? What wants to happen? What are the conditions of my existence now? How am I facing them? What is love's best chance in any of this? *In this and in all the following practices recommended in this book, use art, sculpture, music composition, poetry, dance or any art form that is appealing to you.*

• The question arises: Why do the innocent suffer? This presumes that suffering is a punishment for evil. In the world of the loving Self, there is no punishment, only consequences and opportunities for transformation. To wish that the wicked will suffer is ego-vengeful. To work for their transformation is loving. How have I responded to the evil done to me? What do I feel about punishment, including prison and capital punishment? Do I have a heart that feels sadness for both the victim and the perpetrator? How can I work toward an alternative to the violence of punishment? Is my God an extension of the male punitive ego? Am I creating hell on earth or heaven on earth?

• In Buddhism, there are the Eight Worldly Concerns that challenge our equanimity. To find a path through the center of each set of these dualisms is to be liberated from ego's excessive desire for the positive ones and from its terror of the negative ones: gain and loss, fame and infamy, praise and blame, pleasure and pain. Where do I stand? How can I stand with equipoise and equanimity? How can I extend this poise to others?

• Recite this declaration and notice what you feel about it: It is only when I have the courage to face things as they are, without any self-deception or illusion, that a light will shine from events and a path to contentment will be found. Since all predicaments teach and awaken me, I can be grateful to them all: I do not push my predicament away; I find a way to lean on it. I choose to have no escape hatch. My yes is unconditional: "By the power and truth of this predicament, may all beings have happiness and be free of fear and craving. May I never destroy anyone's happiness. May all people keep choosing the path of peace and cherish all that lives as equally holy. Everything that happens to me is from a sacred heart, a light that will not go out, something unfolding and enfolding. I say yes."

• Create a spiritual safety deposit box, with the key in someone else's hand: ask someone you respect and trust to hold your resolution to act in more healthy ways and to remind you of it if he or she sees you acting contrary to it. For example, you know that you easily involve yourself with predatory partners. Give a friend the right to call you on that choice if it happens again. Your friend is thereby holding the healthy you with all its investments and requirements in safe-keeping and holds the key to it for you.

• Rewrite the following quotations in your own words and then meditate on them very earnestly. Apply each of them to a personal experience in your past or present life:

> *Our ego . . . the neurotic mind that grasps onto a solid sense of self-identity for support, is extremely powerful and will fight against any view that threatens its security. It is deeply disturbed by the suggestion that the I, like everything else, is something merely designated by conceptual thought. Therefore we should expect a lot of resistance when we meditate on the non-self-existence of the I. This is natural; it is only our deeply ingrained ego struggling against annihilation.*
>
> —Lama Yeshe, *Introduction to Tantra:*
> *A Vision of Totality*

> *Perhaps this dread of transience explains our greed for the few gobbets of raw experience in modern life, why violence is libidinous, why lust devours us, why soldiers choose not to forget their days of horror.*
>
> —Peter Matthiessen, *The Snow Leopard*

There is no way to gain emancipation by another.... There is no way to emancipate people from suffering in my world. The only way for you to cross over the raging stream of passion is to know the truth yourself.   —Suttanipata

When one sees eternity in the things that pass away, and infinity in finite things, one has pure knowledge.

—Bhagavad Gita

It is not powerlessness itself that leads to humiliation, but the shock experienced by my pretensions to omnipotence when is comes up against the reality of things. The nature of things is for us the best, the most affectionate, and the most humiliating of masters; it is always around us with its vigilant assistance.

—Hubert Benoit, *Supreme Doctrine: Psychological Studies in Zen Thought*

The Spur of Crisis

The friendlier you are to yourself, the friendlier will your predicament look to you.

Imagine yourself in this situation: You are trapped in a house on fire with only two ways of getting out: you can be pushed from inside, e.g., losing a job or being left by a spouse. You can be pulled from outside, e.g., finding something new for yourself. In either case it will hurt. In either case you will live to go on.

Someone rejects us or leaves us or fires us or dies. We are bereft and unable to handle it well. In such a crisis our ego is finding out that its inflated self-assessments were not valid. Its version of reality was way off. Crisis really means the end of just such an illusion. (The only thing that can be lost is what we had to let go of anyway!) Meister Eckhart says: "Everything is meant to be lost that the soul may stand in unhampered nothingness."

A crisis leads to a discarding. But of what? Only of the shams, disguises, and masks that we were calling our identity. Perhaps now we even see how our relationships or our religion were being used to support the sham. The true Self can emerge only from the surrender of the inflated ego. An ego crisis is weathered successfully when we are different after it. This is being transformed by pain. The pain has been useless if we are back in full control. Jung referred to this as "the regressive restoration of persona." It is putting the old mask back on. It is a refusal to "stand in unhampered nothingness," the only launching pad for a new creation.

The Bible begins with the creation: "The earth was void and darkness covered the deep. The Spirit of God brooded over the waters." Creation myths begin with chaos. Chaos is the given, the condition for something new to emerge. A personal crisis is a microcosm of the primordial chaos and the prerequisite for creativity. When things become topsy-turvy in our life, something is ready to be born in us.

Crisis usually represents a confrontation or an argument with one or more of the conditions of existence. Crisis is a challenge to change. To change is to locate a new level of strength in ourselves and to act in accord with it; to stay unchanged is to regress. There is no middle ground of safety. This is why in a crisis, we enter the void. We see the usual props fail; we see that everything was a prop meant to uphold a shaky ego. In crisis, we feel powerless to maintain the old comfortable structures. We are forced to marshal our strengths and move into something new. Perhaps a grace comes our way: we find strength we did not think we had. We live through the crisis; we are still left standing after the storm. A paradox has appeared: without props, we still stand. What threatens us with breakdown leads to breakthrough.

Traumatic events and crises are familiar. Most of us have felt them since childhood or even infancy. They have imprinted us with stress, anxiety, and uneasiness that are manifest in our bodies, in our sense of who we are, in our way of moving, in our beliefs about our masculinity or femininity, in the way we relate, and even in our physical shape and health. We designed the strategies of a lifetime from the impact of crises and injuries. Our work is to untangle and undo the knots we tied. That task, when handled conscientiously and successfully, makes us kindlier to others and certainly less likely to inflict the same hurts on them. Suffering softens us when we allow it, bear it, and then resolve it and move on.

In adult crisis, we may feel forsaken. This forsakenness is the spiritual equivalent of human betrayal and the withdrawal of our assisting forces. Might the message be: stop looking outside? Can we see the void inside and, in the spaciousness of it, simply sit as fair and alert witnesses of the shambles around us? We might contact our immanence because of our forsakenness. We might find transcendence because of self-limitation. Negatives are necessary in an equation if one is to find the positives on the other side.

In a crisis, our ego often fails us. A crisis is thus an opportunity for a breakthrough of the archetypal world into the ego's dramas. Synchronicity is more observable when the ego is not in the way, since archetypes constellate more strongly as our ego deflates. Has the crisis happened for this reason? "The wind was strong and the sea was rough...when they saw Jesus walking on the water toward their boat" (John 6:19).

A crisis in the hero journey story is meant to precipitate a move. Why the tornado in *The Wizard of Oz?* Dorothy would not have gone otherwise. She tried to leave on her own but was easily persuaded to return, her journey not yet begun. Along comes the crisis, the grace beyond her control that hurls her into her destiny. A crisis can be the spur of the moment, the initiatory pain that leads us out.

We may ask: "Why me?" "Why" is from the vocabulary of reason. Crisis does not hearken to us from that realm. It transcends and defies the rational. It is the chaos that *necessarily* precedes a new creation. Logic and making sense of things are usually impossible to achieve in crisis. Pausing is the proper etiquette. The work of repair is not merely psychological but spiritual: brooding over the troubled waters, not draining them.

Crisis creates tragedy; transformation happens in comedy. To see the humor of a critical event is a fast track to healing. Comedy, like spirituality, unites opposites and thrives on contrast and contradiction. This may be why so many comedies end with a wedding! Humor is often predicated on the ego getting its comeuppance. In comedy, everything is mixed up: decorum and license, prince and pauper, accord and discord, order and disorder, fantasy and reality. Boundaries and identities are tested and stretched. In the comic sense of things, tension is bearable, as in sports, which comfortably combines tension and enjoyment. The sense of humor in comedy defies law and logic. It is at ease with the cross-over of the conceptual to the imaginative: "Methinks I see these things with parted eyes, when everything seems double" (*A Midsummer Night's Dream*). Comedy keeps the promise that in time things will work out, that miracles can happen just in time. In tragedy, it is always too late. In the tragic outcome, the chance for amendment is irretrievably lost. In comedy, all is forgiven and the largesse of this forgiveness leads to amendment. "If you pardon, we will mend" (*A Midsummer Night's Dream*).

A crisis helps us face something about ourselves that we have been overlooking. If we look carefully, we might see that all the crises and issues of our lives go back to a central fear. For example, we may believe that vulnerability will lead to being dropped. We may resolve that fear by choosing to *dive!* There is an archetypal dimension to this — now familiar — theme and it helps us to know more about daring to free ourselves from fear. In pagan times, a dive was considered a conscious baptism: a plunge of the ego into the waters that dissolve it. Diving is a symbol of daring the death of the ego and of its frantic clinging to fear and desire. To resurface from the water is to be reborn in the likeness of the Self, purified of attachment. A Hindu scripture says that the sea dissolves our name, i.e., our exclusive identification with ego.

A leap is a metaphor for the combination of opposites: risk and surrender. Diving represents a readiness for total letting go — without having to be pushed. It is heroic because it is voluntary. Diving off a very high cliff was a sacrament in ancient Greece and Turkey. This was the order of the rite: Myths about heroes and their feats were read aloud by the priest. This made the ancestral heroes present as assisting forces and encouraging advocates to the diver. An intoxicating herb was given to the diver to make it easier to dare the leap into the waters awaiting him. The diver dove off the cliff. His life flashed before him as he sailed through the air, as if it were being reviewed for the last time and then ended. The gods' grace supported him and, by identifying with it, he emerged reborn from the waters to the cheers of the people.

Diving also became associated with proofs of daring or caring. Pliny says that Sappho, an excellent diver, dove from a cliff in Lesbos "to transcend earthly love." Throughout history, from China to New England, the ritual plunge became a universal judicial ordeal to prove one's innocence or one's favor with God. Christian baptism is a plunge into the waters that bring the death of the old Adam (ego) and the rebirth of the new Christ (Self) in the human soul. It is a sacrament in that it is a correlation of a ritual and a grace, an act with a result that matches it, hence synchronicity.

In the Greek rite, women stood on the sidelines and encouraged the men to dive. This is an archetypal role of the feminine: to help drown the male ego. The Sirens, Lorelei, and mermaids are personifications of this seduction into dissolution — a role women have played archetypally for centuries. Men today may have noticed it happening in their relationship with women too! In our relationships, we may be willing to live together, to love, to be faithful. Are we willing to risk this other plunge into the dissolving of our ego? If only we trusted that when ego goes, all our fears go with it. Fear dives in but it is brave love that climbs out.

If there is a fear of falling, the only safety is in deliberately jumping.
                                                        — Carl Jung

PRACTICE

• To keep us on our toes and to maintain homeostasis, events occur that shake us up or cool us down. Everything that happens to us, every person who comes along in our lives, every success, failure, betrayal. or loyalty is meant not to debilitate us but to empower us. Only through such a variety of experiences of all of life's options can we reach our potential for showing unconditional love, perennial wisdom, and healing power. We can work with this elegantly or be dragged to it kicking and screaming.

• Write an inventory of all the times you went along with events in life and all the times you fought them. List the persons and events. How has each helped you become who you are? How have any tried to obstruct you?

• Read this aloud: When tragedy strikes in my life, I am tempted to ask: "What did I do to deserve this?" This is a normal guilt reaction with roots in childhood superstition. An adult — and more highly evolved — spiritual alternative is presented to me: *This is not about what I did. This is about what I am called to be.* This way of configuring it is in keeping with the relationship between synchronicity and destiny. Everything that happens is about how I am called to be all that I can be, not about how bad I was or how victimized I am. How have the tragedies in my life opened the door to new vistas, helped me find my own truth, led me to show more love, and made me more compassionate toward and understanding of others? When I focus on these questions, I make what has happened workable in the ongoing unfolding of my heroic story.

• Nothing is so discouraging as the point at which we are stymied or stuck in dilemmas and no decision seems possible. But the stymied point, the stuckness is the pause: the "mysterious pass through the apparently impenetrable mountains," described in the Tao. I am not stuck but released when I go into that gap. I am released from my ego's dualisms. As I trust this space and relax into it, something will automatically change and I will know my next step with intuitive ease. Inner space is simply my potential. As I enter the pause, the mysterious pass in the lost hills, all the old habitual conceptions of myself disappear and in their silent place there remains the divine light that I have always and already been. This divinity is the fully activated potential of myself. God is the archetype of this profound awakening to my true identity.

Can I tolerate my emotional reactions without being overwhelmed by them? I sometimes feel myself collapsing under the weight of my concerns or problems. I can decide to hold my disintegration rather than try to escape from it or fix it. I can hold my terrifying feelings as I hold a child with a terrifying nightmare. Simply by holding and cradling her, I help her regain her reason and be soothed. I can hold myself that way, and thereby reconstitute myself. I can hold my own disintegration till it becomes integrated. The belief that restitution will follow disruption leads to a sense of trust in the universe and in the cohesive strength within me. Feelings then become signs of lively tides, not of tidal waves. I find myself forming the psychic structures and then performing the healthy functions of the functional ego. "Hold the sadness and pain of Samsara in your heart and at the same time the power and vision of the great Eastern sun. Only then can the warrior make a proper cup of tea!" says Trungpa Rinpoche. (*Samsara* is the enticing but transitory world of desire.) I say to myself (and/or my partner):

> You can be broken down and I will hold and love you that way.

> You can fall apart and I will hold and love you that way.

> You can have nothing to offer for now and I will hold and love you that way.

> You can be at your lowest ebb and I will hold and love you that way.

You can be depressed, contorted, wounded or distraught and I will hold and love you that way.

I will do this with no insistence that you be fixed. I can accommodate a you that breaks down and is not available for my needs for the time being.

Write a poem about this potential and actual power in yourself for self-restorative emotional thriving.

• I look at my present intimate relationship and notice how it nurtures me or depletes or even abuses me. I contemplate my partner and picture him/her in the romance phase of our relationship and then in the conflict stage. I see him/her with compassion. I articulate my truth about my partner and my commitment to him/her directly.

• Here are some rules of thumb that may be helpful in discovering and embracing your own reality. Following these may help you know who you really are and then know how to act on that knowledge in healthy ways:

- Tell those close to you what you feel within yourself and in reaction to them, no matter how embarrassing it may be.

- If necessary, allow yourself to retreat from a distressing issue long enough to regroup your strengths. Then come back and face the music with a sense of personal power.

- Stop and hold every feeling, cradling it and allowing it to have its full career in you. Distractions and avoidances only conceal you from yourself. We learned early in life to overlook. We overlooked our own feelings so as not "to hurt the feelings" of others. This stop and hold method reverses that misguided self-sacrifice.

- Embrace this program for handling fear: admit your fear, allow yourself to feel it, and then act as if it were not able to stop you.

Some fears are obstacles to what you really want. Other fears are signals that you are attempting something that you do not want. For example, you may fear commitment to a partner. If that fear is a hurdle to jump in your own evolution, apply the program above to *fulfill* your authentic needs and wishes. If that fear is a warning to you that you are not cut out for a committed relationship but only for lighter ones, then take the fear as *information* about your authentic needs and wishes. How can you tell the difference? Let the record speak: How have you mostly operated — as opposed to how you have wished to operate — in relationships? What has mostly worked? Fear thrives on isolation, trappedness, and powerlessness. Admitting fear reduces ego and ends isolation in favor of connection with and support by others. (Actually, the more deeply personal a feeling is, the more definitely can you trust that it is universally felt!) Allowing fear turns it into excitement and suddenly reveals an alternative. Acting bravely brings empowerment and raises self-esteem.*

• Here are three pegs of self-esteem: The first is to act in the most loving way you can toward everyone. The second is to have a sense of accomplishment based on your doing all you can with your talents and potential. (This will usually require discipline and patience as you learn what you need to know and gain the credentials you need to have to do the work you find your bliss in.) The third is to grant yourself the freedom to live in accord with your deepest wishes and needs and to act in accord with them. (This is the secret of finding out who you really are!) Here are some ways of knowing what these wishes and needs are:

• Free yourself from inhibition and clinging.

• Tell the truth about yourself. Self-disclosure leads to self-knowing.

---

*See David Richo, *When Love Meets Fear: How to Become Defense-Less and Resource-Full* (Paulist Press, 1997).

- Ask often for what you already know you want and gradually you will ask yourself — and others — for the deeper things.

- Set boundaries in your relationships and you will know a great deal about yourself and your real needs. In a truly healthy relationship, you do not have to submerge, deny, or kill off any of your deepest needs and wishes.

- Examine what makes you happy and gives you a sense of fulfillment.

- Explore what you do that flows from blissful choice and what is based on a sense of obligation or habit. Resolution: "I will make no choices or promises that repudiate my deepest needs and wishes."

- Look at the record: the history of what you have actually done in the course of your life tells you more about yourself than the fantasy of what you wish you had done or what you say you want.

- Think about how your life would be different if you acted with the highest level of consciousness, health, and spirituality. The difference probably reveals what you truly want and need.

- Consider that the qualities of people you strongly admire may be ones that you want — and can have too.

- Realize that what you want for your children and best friends may tell you what you want.

- Consider the ingredients of your present life, e.g., relationship, housing, job, friends, diet, etc. Plot yourself on the following spectrum to see just how much your choices reflect your deepest wishes: indifference, interest, enthusiasm, excitement.

- Make an inventory of your fears. On the other side of the coin of fear is an excitement/risk that is unlived. There lie our disenfranchised feelings, wishes, and needs.

- Ask where your dreams and synchronicity lead you.

Respond to each of the entries in the above list, noticing which feelings, wants, values, and needs come through most frequently.

- Some of our difficulty in finding out who we are and what we need stems from toxic injunctions and imperatives that we have introjected. We heard or imbibed perspectives from our parents and others that interrupted our self-emergence. These may have taken the form of verbal messages that negated our power, beliefs that diminished or inhibited us, images of what a man or woman *should* be.

These three forms of childhood detritus may now litter our psyche so that we cannot walk freely toward our personal destiny. They are generalized myths that do not fit our individual reality. They are to be examined and scuttled if they do not serve us, if they disable us, or if they render us powerless. Only those messages, beliefs, and images that animate our potential and release it are to be cherished and maintained. Obedience to self-defeating messages, beliefs, and images denies us the chance to be who we are. In such obedience we cannot love ourselves, part of which is allowing ourselves to live in accord with our deepest needs and wishes.

A belief system that has despair as its bottom line may be organizing our life experiences and choices. "I am fated to lose," "Nothing I do will ever work out," "I'll never be good enough." These *sentences* do not arise from what is truly ourselves but from an alien cargo that may have been smuggled into our psyches in early life. Before we could discriminate, our parents' worst fears and beliefs may have been stowaways in our minds. To maintain the crucially needed tie with our parents, we may have had to join them in their despair about us or themselves. This happened at the dear price of our own self-authenticated experience of the world. Now optimistic glimmers, encouraging signs, hopeful prospects, and even kind words or compliments fall flat. They land in the quicksand of automatic repudiation and disavowal.

Despair is the illusion that there is an inexorable fate that awaits our condition and our enterprises. Synchronicity tells us there is no such thing as an inexorable fate. Choices continue to arise and paths continue to appear even until the eleventh hour of a lifetime. Even if the path is to grieve an ending, the next step is to go on. Even if it is our ending, are we not still able to salute the sunset with dignity, equanimity, and deeply contented serenity?

Look at the choices you have made: Were they based on the messages, beliefs, and images of others or of yourself? Have you looked at them consciously and then deliberately chosen them? Are you carrying someone else's myth, an alien presence inside? The work is to clear yourself of false and self-defeating myths. Do this by looking at the record: What has worked for you, i.e., what has led to bliss and success? What has failed? Which of these has been scuttled and which has been maintained?

Pip loved life and all life's peaceable securities, so that the panic-striking business in which he had become entrapped, had most sadly burned his brightness, tho, as ere long would be seen, what was thus temporarily subdued in him, in the end was destined to be illumined by strange wild fires, that showed him off to ten times the natural lustre with which in his native Connecticut, he had once enlivened many a fiddlers' frolic on the green, and at melodious even-tide, with his gay Ha, Ha! had turned the round horizon into one star-belled tambourine.   —Herman Melville, *Moby Dick*

Guides Who Come to Wave Us On

Although I showed you the path to liberation, you must walk it alone.   —Buddha

The hero acknowledges that his own capacities and efforts are inadequate to the full requirements of his task. He consults the archetype of the trusted advisor, i.e., wisdom, in the form of a wise old man or woman. This is the spiritual yearning to hear a numinous voice, to make contact with the infinite, to ask for the grace that takes us beyond the limitations of our own knowledge and powers. It is not about seeking answers to mundane questions. It is an acknowledgment that we will always have to look beyond ourselves to find ourselves.

Assisting forces continually appear in history and in our daily life. They take many forms: people, writings, animals, etc. Scriptures like the Vedas, the Bible, and the Koran are examples of guides. They are limitless wisdom submitting to the limits of time and space: a kind of incarnation. The teachings mirror the wisdom of the Self, which is why they are recognizable as wise. Since this is so, the teachings exist from the beginning of time. Teachers or gurus are legitimate as channels because they are in a line of succession to that beginning. A guide is an incarnation of the archetype of assistance. To a true teacher, the teachings are the teacher.

Animals, both when we are awake and in our dreams, also serve as guides. Jung said: "When we become more spiritual, an animal appears." Animals may appear in life experience and in dreams, at synchronous times, to accompany or even escort us along our path. Joseph Campbell writes: "Animals are the great shamans and teachers,...messengers signaling some wonder,...one's own personal guardian come to bestow its warning and protection." Animals sometimes appear synchronously when we need information about our path. This is referred to as animal medicine. I absently look out of a high window wondering if it is time to let go of my relationship. Suddenly, out of nowhere, two hummingbirds come directly to the window, where they do not ordinarily appear. This is "hummingbird medicine" that may be saying: "Give it a little longer!" An eagle feather falls at my feet as I am fearing to take a certain risk. This is "eagle medicine," perhaps encouraging me to boldness. The synchronicity is in the unexpected and unusual placement of the animal, the timeliness of its appearance, and the precision of the metaphor.

A person who is a true guide has characteristics like these:

• She is a trusted advisor who asks for respectful attention, not blind obedience.

• He is an escort to our unique destiny. To honor our guide evokes his power to show us the path, protect us, and even give us the grace of an impetus from which there is no turning back.

• A guide may also be one who reveals — or challenges — the meaning of the flora and fauna of the path: cryptic messages of the unconscious.

• A true guide never looks for ego enhancement or asserts her ego over others. She leads us beyond our own egos because she has already transcended it in herself. She never takes advantage of us physically, emotionally, sexually, financially, or in any other way.

• A valid guide always leads us back to ourselves and the riches within us. He does not want to be clung to as a source, but only be attended to as a channel. He empowers us to find the power in us. Buddha uses the analogy of the raft for his teachings. A raft is provisional; it works to get us across the river, but then it is meant to be left behind so that we can walk unencumbered through our own jungle. The best teachings/teacher are those we can leave safely at the threshold of what comes next for us on our journey. The teachings, like the raft, bring us to where the journey begins. It is our task to enlist new forces from within so we can continue on our path. (Nevertheless, carrying along a book as a vademecum is a shrewd move!)

• Our freedom to choose is an indispensable ingredient for our work of opening ourselves to wholeness. A true guide cherishes and is immensely sensitive to our freedom. She gingerly offers external supports only as a means of activating our inner resources, not as replacements of them. She wants us to have our own life, not be dependent on her.

The guide is often a stranger, of another creed or nationality, e.g., the dwarfs in Snow White. Another example is in the Hasidic story of the Czech rabbi who dreams of a treasure buried under a bridge. He does not find the treasure there but a guard in Prague tells his own dream to the rabbi, mockingly saying he saw a treasure in a rabbi's house under the hearth. Note how the guard/guide also ridicules the meaningfulness of dreams. Our guide, too, may point by laughing. As we become friendlier to bedrock reality, that reality itself appears more and more as the true guide, ever presenting opportunities for initiation. Unadorned reality gives us our best instruction on the path. Our pretensions to sovereignty collapse in the implacable face of this invincible governor. He seems to abolish us over and over but only to fulfill us once and for all.

In Coleridge's poem *The Rime of the Ancient Mariner*, the mariner killed the albatross and brought bad luck upon himself and the crew. He became an afflicting force when every sailor has to be an assisting force. The albatross was a bird of good omen that led ships through icy waters. The mariner unconsciously shot down a spiritual guide, a visionary grace that was meant to complement sailors' ego efforts on their voyage toward wholeness. It is in us archetypally to deny and kill the powers that come to help or love or complete us. The mariner has found no way to make up for his misdeed. Death and loneliness reign. He is condemned to wear the lifeless albatross around his neck. He sits alone one night and simply gazes in wrapt attention at the sea and its marvelous creatures. He is attending and staying: mindfulness! In this *effortless* moment, the mariner's "kind saint" takes pity on him and he blesses the creatures he feared before. "A spring of love gushed,"

"my kind saint," "unaware," are all ways of showing the effortless and hence egoless nature of the experience. It is pure grace.
It happens to and through the mariner and at that moment "the
albatross fell off, and sank like lead into the sea." We have only
to sit and watch the show. Assisting forces come into play: "my
kind saint" releases a spring from my heart and frees something
from my neck — and through this intervention of grace, healing
happens. The mariner is the ego; the kind saint is the Self. They
can be good friends when we have lost our way and our egos
offer no navigation.

*How do I rely on my own effort and imagine that it is all there
is? How do I kill what most I love or need? How do I carry the
albatross of my past mistakes? What will it take to let it go?
How do I welcome my assisting forces? How do I deny them
entry?*

•

An allegorical guide figure is a *shaman*. He serves as a mediator
between the visible and the invisible worlds. He is a healer and a
seer, the central assisting force in a tribal community, a personification of grace. His vocation comes from a tutelary spirit and
from its helper-spirits and cannot be refused. The calling often
begins with a wound that is mysteriously healed. The shaman
undergoes an initiation of pain or even dismemberment. His survival is then the reenactment of the death-resurrection theme. The
shaman learns the art of traveling easily from the earthly to the
heavenly plane. He ascends with humankind's prayers and de-
scends with divine messages. This is a metaphor for the axis of the
profane and the sacred in human integration. Since the shaman
partakes of both the world of appearances and the world of spirit,
he can resist mortal pain at will, e.g., walk on hot coals and converse freely with divine beings. The shaman is a sherpa to the
beyond, a guide who knows the itinerary to the immortal world.
His ability to fly is the metaphor of this wisdom about higher
things. A Veda says: "Those who know have wings!" The shaman

transcends the human condition and the community reveres him
and looks to him as an advocate for its survival. Actually, what
they feel is nostalgia, since everyone had these powers in the archaic past but lost them as ego gained ascendancy. *The Egyptian
Book of the Dead* described the soul as a falcon that flies away
to the primordial garden. The "original fall" is from this flying
condition.

Sacraments and rituals rebuild the bridge between heaven and
earth, reviving communication with the spirit world, and reconciling human beings and gods. The shaman crosses this bridge,
bringing candidates with him once they are ready. The bridge is
open "only for an instant" (the synchronous moment, the *kairos,*
the mysterious pass).

These intriguing metaphors describe our capacity to transcend
opposites, to move beyond the limits of our senses and our sen-
sibility, and to abolish the polarities of time and timelessness.
Shamanism is an abiding promise of a passageway between the
warring oppositions that the ego thrives on. This is where nature's
laws no longer limit us and freedom becomes immediately possible. The shamanic powers are in the Self and become available to
us when we build the bridge between it and the healthy ego. We
then fly to spiritual heights and transcend the limits of the time-
bound world. Synchronicity is the mediator of this, the familiar
shamanic advocate that assists us in the passage from dismem-
bered ego to wholeness. This is the genuine passage to our own
authentic being with its own flight patterns, its own sighs, and its
own unexpected miracles.

> *The deer on the evergreen mountain*
> *Where there are no fallen leaves,*
> *Can know the coming of autumn*
> *Only by its own cry.*
>
> — Yoshinobu, 900 C.E.

PRACTICE

Who are the guides in your life? How are you thanking them? How have you listened or not listened to their suggestions? Do the people you consider guides fit the criteria outlined above? How do dreams and synchronicities act as guides and shamans for you?

Guidance does not end with death. Enlightened saints and Bodhisattvas remain to help us as we struggle on. Their love, wisdom, and healing did not die with them but live on in the treasury from which we draw every moment of every day. St. John Chrysostom wrote in his hymn to Mary on the day of her ascent from earth to heaven: "You went away, but you never left us!" Express appreciation to the sources of invisible assistance in your life. If there is ever someone you respect who is about to die, consider asking him or her to be your guide from the next plane for the rest of your life. Ask this also of someone already passed over, especially someone who really loved you.

> *The terrifying darkness had become complete.... Suddenly, my room blazed with an indescribably white light. I was seized with an ecstasy beyond description.... I stood upon the summit of a mountain where a great wind blew. A wind not of air but of spirit. In great, clean strength, it blew right through me. Then came the blazing thought, "You are a free man"... A great peace stole over me and... I became acutely conscious of a Presence which seemed like a veritable sea of living spirit. I lay on the shores of a new world.... For the first time, I felt that I really belonged. I knew that I was loved and could love in return.*
>
> —Bill Wilson, founder of Alcoholics Anonymous,
> a program based on the guidance of a power higher than the ego

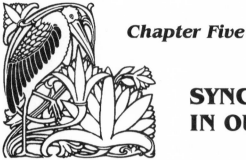

Chapter Five

SYNCHRONICITY IN OUR DREAMS

In dreams, the psyche speaks in images, and gives expression to instincts which derive from the most primitive level of nature. Therefore, through the assimilation of unconscious contents, the momentary life of consciousness can once more be brought into harmony with the law of nature, from which it all too easily departs, and we can be led back to the natural law of our own being.
                                                              — Carl Jung

Myths are metaphors of our human potentials. Dreams are mythic stories that capture our attention, an attention that can lead to healing. Dreams, poetry, and myths all emerge from the same place: the point of contact between spirit and matter, human and divine, male and female, personal and transpersonal, ego and Self. These are all related as Yin to Yang: complementaries that are ultimately unities (like breathing in and out). Dreams are the royal road to and from the unconscious. They reveal our identity, our path, our next step, what resides in us and is ready to speak. Each dream speaks to our condition. Since dreams thus reflect and presage our life predicaments, they are living examples of synchronicity.

To know who we are is a twofold task. It is first of all to know our deepest wishes and longings as well as our loves and fears. It is also to know the space that opens in us when we go beyond needs, wishes, and fears, and expand our love. Dreams show us how to move between one and the other, how to continue our journey. Dreams introduce us not only to parts of ourselves but to visiting archetypes who may come to free us from the domination of the ego.

Our ego identity is encrusted with habitual ways of seeing ourselves, others, and our life. It is supremely devoid of surprises, full of boring, hackneyed, and predictable responses. Our soul identity is free of habits, biases, and orthodoxy. It is full of surprises, full of grace. Within this spiritual identity is a set of accurate, appropriate, and courageous responses to whatever life may bring. Our true Self is a reliable inner repertory of powers. It is like a Swiss army knife with blades for every circumstance that may face us in the forest. Dreams come to us from this power place — or rather space — in us.

Our journey is to advance past our ego's entrenchments long enough to feel contact with wholeness in our soul/universe. Dreams are visions from a superior intelligence that points out our ego's blind spots and challenges us to deal with them. Dreams come from a knowledge larger than ego or I.Q. They tell us what we do not yet know. We have minds that are unable to know the deepest truths about us. What we figure out mentally about the meaning of a dream often misses the mark because dreams speak the soul's language to the ego. They are not ego talking to itself. Like angels, dreams are intelligent agents that come to help us. Decisions made on the basis of logic alone betray this soulful voice within us that, thanks to our dreams, will not be silent long.

Dreams do not tell us what to do but what is unlived in us. This larger intelligence is unconscious and does not use logic or clear language. The soul is the dream-maker, not the logical mind. According to Jung, the soul is the connecting link between our consciousness and our unconscious. Soul is made up of images. The unconscious produces images as the body produces T-cells: pictures that tell how healing happens and even make it happen.

Dreams and synchronicity work together most conspicuously
in what Jung calls the transcendent function of the psyche: a healing, synthesizing image arises automatically in a dream when we
hold our warring tensions rather than side with any one of them.
When we hold, rather than attach ourselves to one polarity, opposites combine. For example, we notice we are overly controlling
and yet also at times overly submissive. To hold both of these is
to contemplate both of them, to make room for them by accepting their equal legitimacy but not acting solely from one or the
other. A healing third option will arise: I see myself in a dream
being gentle and yet still asserting my rights. In this image — and
consequent plan to put it into action — my quandary is resolved.
I respect both sides and find a way to show both sides without vi-
olating myself or anyone else. This is how chaos becomes cosmos.
The psyche synchronously produces just the image that helps us
reconcile our inner oppositions. We face a conflict at the same
time that the psyche provides a solution. Butterflies were the most
common image on the walls of the children's camps in Nazi Germany. What a touching example of the transcendent function of
the beleaguered psyche!

Dreams show our conscious ego: where it is on its journey,
where it has become one-sided, where changes want to happen.
The face we hide from in the daylight turns back to us in dreams.
What we have excluded, i.e., do not believe we can integrate,
now demands inclusion since the psyche has powerful instinc-
tive directedness: it wants to include and integrate everything split
off by fear and resistance. We fear anything unknown. We fear
and resist our dark side full of dangerous impulses and our light
side full of potentials for good. Synchronously, a dream brings an
image that speaks to this condition. There is a unique meaning in
this unique image in our unique life for our unique destiny.

Dreams come from the divine nucleus of psyche to the orbit-
ing electrons of daily life. When we listen to our dreams, they
take us deeper into the fertile terrain of the Self. Deeper means:
a more meaningful and harmonious connection between ego and

Self, i.e., more soul. To say that dreams have no meaning is like being in Turkey and believing that the language spoken there is gibberish. At the same time, dreams are not to be taken literally or as giving total information. Sometimes they are like a compass, showing where North is but not how to get there or what will be there when we arrive. Yet, at other times, they are like a map that shows exactly how to get there. *Am I willing to go?*

> *Dreams prepare, announce, or warn about situations long before they happen. This is not a miracle or precognition. Most crises have a long incubation in the unconscious.*
>
> — Carl Jung

How to Remember Dreams

Interest and focus are the two keys to a good memory. This applies to remembering dreams. The more you pay attention to the process of remembering, the more you remember. The more effort you put into remembering, the more you will remember. "Attention to the unconscious pays it a compliment that guarantees its cooperation," says Jung.

• Use autosuggestion throughout the day and while falling asleep: "I am remembering my dreams, waking up, and writing them down."

• Keep a pad and pen or recorder by the bed, planning to use them upon awakening from each dream during the night. You will easily fall back to sleep.

• Avoid sharp body movements. These tend to jostle short-term memory.

• Wake up naturally, without an alarm.

• Keep a dream journal in which you write dreams out in full detail. Upon awakening during the night, write only key phrases that summarize the dream.

• Use a sense exercise: picture a dream image in your mind, then move it, smell it, listen to its sounds, notice its surroundings.

• As you awaken, keep your eyes closed after a dream lest you be seduced and distracted by objects in the bedroom. With your eyes closed, review key elements in the dream and then jot them down.

• The more you drop the need for an explanation, the more you access the dream world beyond the ordinary ego-mind.

• Review these dream categories to remember a dream: *Characters:* friends, family, famous, mythic, strangers? *Nature:* tree, birds, stars, water, etc.? *Objects:* clothes, weapons, tools, buildings, etc.? *Emotions:* joy, anger, fear, grief, compassion? *Sensations:* warmth, cold, senses? *Setting:* home, work, theater, church, indoors, outdoors, strange/familiar, etc.? solitary? silent? *Modifiers:* small, big, ugly, etc.? *Outcomes:* fail, win, resolved, unresolved, happy, unhappy? *Interactions:* fight, play, cooperate, compete, sex?

• Once a dream is remembered, tell or write the dream in the present tense. Give the dream a title and a one-sentence summary. Make note of the context of the day. Notice where the dream fits in a series of dreams with similar themes. Notice colors, textures, smells (All dreams are in color, but color is forgotten first. It is useful to make note of colors first when you recall and write a dream.) Treat each object as individual, not general (*this* lynx, not *a* lynx) and as alive: there is lively energy in every person, place, or thing in a dream. Associate from each image (what does this lead me to think of?). Identify with images and characters (play each part). Every person and thing may be a part of me not yet integrated. Converse with images and characters in an inner dialogue. Finish imaginatively what is unfinished in the dream. Notice what was left out and bring it in. Answer unanswered questions. Experiment with different endings and notice the feelings that follow.

• Pay attention to setting, bodily and emotional reactions. What may this dream be compensating for? Distinguish objective meanings (family members or significant others appearing in picture perfect form usually represent themselves) from subjective meanings (dream figures who are strangers or "it looked like Ma but was not"; these are often symbols of parts of ourselves that ask for attention or integration).

Ask yourself these questions: What part of me feels like that? What place feels like that place? What in my life makes me feel like that? What needs to be let go of? taken hold of? What part of me am I abandoning, fearing, rejecting? How is my life like this? See objects and events of the day as direct addresses to you, as assisting and afflicting forces.

Use the above techniques also in daily life to ground yourself in situations that may seem strange or surreal.

• Dreams are meant to be lived with as friends, not analyzed as patients. We gain more from a dream when we allow it to reveal itself to us rather than when we try to interpret it and pin it down to one meaning. No dream has a single meaning. The meaning of a dream may change with time. Let the dream unfold itself. I see my cat sitting on a chair. I can wonder when she will jump off. I can insist on answering this question and even become agitated by the suspense. Or I can simply keep observing her, and sooner or later I will see her jump and then I will know when she jumped. Can I be this patient with my dream, allowing it to leap to me with meaning when it is ready?

• The fact that an image in a dream is the same as or related to something that happened the day before does not mean that its significance is less potent. The dream-maker is a casting director using any people, things, or events to tell your story. Dreams are not literal but rather metaphorical and symbolic. The symbolism is not diminished by the familiarity of the images any more that a film is any less meaningful simply because it stars a familiar actor.

• There is no morality in dreams. Stealing, for instance, may mean relocating energy to make it ready for a new use. Hermes and Prometheus stole to help humankind. They live as archetypes in us, as do all the heroes and villains we have met in fact and fiction.

• Interpretation is suspicious if it coincides with expectation, since the unconscious is compensatory, not parallel, to our wishes or needs.

• Never accept "I don't know!" Find the place in you where knowledge waits to be discovered. Make up something and see how it fits.

• "I saw a dog but then he turned into a man." The first form is usually meant to lead to the more significant form.

• Pay most attention to what engages, disgusts, or puzzles you most.

• If you are self-destructive in a dream, ask yourself what in your ego may be blocking development.

• An isolated sense in a dream may mean a unique development not yet shared by or showable to others. Recall that any higher consciousness is often a form of loneliness, since those around you may not grasp what you have grasped.

• The more active you are in a dream, the more involved are you in your conscious process, e.g., "I planted flowers" vs. "I saw flowers being planted."

• It is a sign of progress when dreams no longer use symbols for feelings (e.g., fire for anger) but feelings occur in the dream directly.

• "I had a bad dream." There are no bad dreams. "Bad" shows what something unlived or unacknowledged looks like inside you. You are finding out not how bad you are but how badly some part of you wants to be exposed and dealt with.

• "I must be a terrible person and have such evil things in me to have such dreams!" All of us contain all the images of humankind. All of us have the whole human shadow inside. "Yet in thy dark streets shineth an everlasting light...." There is a creative kernel in every dark image, a potential for light and goodness. It appears when we stop seeing ourselves as bad.

• Dreams work with synchronicity because they confirm or

challenge steps and transitions on our soul-journey. They do this by foretelling the future, sending or receiving information before the mind can know it, and presenting the very images that help us find our path or change it. In this sense, all images are assisting forces. In dreams, as in synchronicity, opposites unite and paradox reigns. This follows from the fact that the psyche is a balanced whole which transcends logical distinction. Synchronicity and dreams balance the ego's exaggerations and its unlived, disowned characteristics. Dreams and synchronicity compensate for the biases of the ego and can rectify them too. Dreams work with synchronicity also through a series of dreams. Reading one's dream journal can make the apparently inchoate assemblage of recent dreams suddenly coherent. Specific themes or images appear more than once and point to a more orderly proceeding than one might have suspected. This is the inner shaping of individuation. Dreamwork — the techniques above and the ones that will follow — shapes it externally.

Recurrent Dreams

The "Zeigarnik effect" is a theory stating that an uncompleted task returns to memory and presses for completion, whereas completed tasks are quiet. This is how recurrent dreams can point to a continuing defect or excess that clamors for attention. They may also indicate a trauma not yet assimilated. The image is repeated in dreamland to help us absorb and integrate its far-flung shock. Recurrent dreams can also anticipate a development in the psyche. They are recurrent because something wants to come in: "Who knocks so loudly?" (*Romeo and Juliet*).

Common examples of recurrent dream themes include: a fear of falling, a car that will not start or stop, unpreparedness for an exam, rescuing of a child, cataclysm, lateness, inability to leave, inability to get in, exclusion, nudity, animals.

Dream places are also important, in accord with the ancient belief that healing is often associated with specific places: Asclepian temples, Ganges, Machu Picchu, Lourdes.*

Keep track of the dream themes or images that recur each time you begin a new enterprise. This may help you know whether an upcoming decision is a good one. For example: you notice that the image of a car that will not start has appeared in your dream journal before enterprises that have failed. Perhaps that image is a caution about a choice that is coming up.

Synchronicity and recurrent dreams are linked when they both seem to declare the same message. I may have a series of dreams in which I am losing my grip and then suffer a diminution of my powers in my conscious life. Dreams will often confirm or deny a choice that I have made and that has great consequences. Since the external and internal worlds are two sides of a single coin of consciousness, the world of action and the world of dreams actively unite.

In times of strong feeling, the psyche will produce an archetypal image. This is synchronicity. The unconscious spontaneously produces images in dreams or even in consciousness. This is synchronicity. The psyche channels images from the treasury of soul, both personal and archetypal, to produce living symbols that reconcile either/ors, show us where our work is, and produce healing that leads to individuation. This is synchronicity. The psyche has a complete lexicon of images both from our life experience and from our ancestors, and it knows exactly which one fits this occasion. This is how our soul and its synchronicity is helping us do our work. To work a conflict through in one's inner life leads to less need to obsess about it or dramatize it in one's daily life. This

---

*Here is a curious and touching witness by the Dalai Lama: "... my visit to Lourdes last year as a pilgrim. There, in front of the cave, I experienced something very special. I felt a spiritual vibration, a kind of spiritual presence there. And then in front of the image of the Virgin Mary, I prayed, I expressed my admiration for this holy place that has long been a source of inspiration and strength, that has provided spiritual solace, comfort, and healing to millions of people. And I prayed that this might continue for a long time to come" (*The Good Heart: A Buddhist Perspective on the Teachings of Jesus* [Boston: Wisdom, 1996], p. 84).

is because we focus on that center in ourselves where images are generated and where opposites are reconciled. As we relate to our own ego-transcending center, we make visible the wholeness that is already and always in us.

Archetypal Dreams

Whenever we contact the deeper archetypal reality of the psyche, it permeates us with a feeling of being in touch with the infinite. — Marie-Louise Von Franz

Archetypes are recurrent typical themes of the human psyche that appear as images or characters in stories and myths. The archetypes are fields of psychic energy within the Self. They propose a spiritual challenge to the ego: to live out each of its dimensions. These include the hero, the shadow, the wise guide, the trickster. Individuation happens as we consciously integrate these unconscious drives — or instincts — toward wholeness. Wholeness is in fact the integration of all the archetypal potentials within us.

Most dreams come from our personal unconscious and tell us about our ego work, i.e., how to function in the world so that we can relate effectively. This is our psychological challenge. A few come from our collective, cosmic unconscious and declare an archetypal task, i.e., a spiritual challenge. Archetypes or archetypal images come to meet us in a dream, carrying with them a grace or power to assist us in our conscious choices. This visit has a numinous quality; it is a spiritual vision that beckons us onward and empowers us on our human trek toward wholeness.

Archetypal dreams grant us a glimpse of the invisible world. They demonstrate the priority of spirituality. Miracles are constant in the psyche, a realm where nature's laws are not obeyed and ego limits are transcended. Archetypal dreams are thus initiation rites into our spiritual work. Archetypal dreams occur in moments of crisis. They herald a transition, a time when a new strength is ready to surface or a new attitude is required to meet new challenges. The old or one-sided attitude no longer suffices. Oracular, ego-transcending wisdom of the archetypal Self emerges from deep in the psyche. The Delphic priestess has always been sitting here inside us, but we never traveled far enough within ourselves to consult her. Archetypal dreams are in her now ready-to-be-audible voice.

How can we tell the difference between archetypal and personal dreams? Archetypal dreams unfold like a hero story, a journey, a struggle, a discovery. There is a sense of channeling, as if the dream came from a realm far beyond us. We may feel a power that contains us; we do not contain it. Synchronicities abound in waking life to match the motifs of such dreams. Strong feeling characterizes the dreams and the memory of them. In fact, archetypal dreams are unforgettable — unlike many personal dreams. There is a strong sense of the numinous (otherworldly) in the dream. Archetypal dreams lead directly to transformation. For example, I may dream that I am drowning in a vast and turbulent sea. Suddenly, a ghostly woman appears. She is hovering over the water beckoning to me to join her. I say that I cannot manage that. A dolphin then arises and leaps up to her, splashing me with such force that I now seem doomed for certain. I awake with fear and the sense that an opportunity to go beyond my habitual limits has been missed. I recognize the woman as a force of feminine power that challenges my reluctant consciousness and even offers me new powers and perspectives (in the form of the dolphin). I keep pondering this dream throughout the day. What flying leaps am I afraid to take? What assisting force am I not hopping onto? What voice am I saying no to? What waters of rebirth am I allowing to drown me? How can I grab onto the dolphin's tail?

Dreamwork

Jung wrote: "Dreamwork releases an experience that grips or falls upon us as from above, an experience that has substance and body such as those things which occurred to the ancients. If I were to symbolize it, I would choose the Annunciation." The Annunciation to Mary by the angel Gabriel is an archetype of the tidings of destiny. This scene conveys in one instant the integration of our psychological and spiritual work. Mary says yes unconditionally to her destiny and becomes pregnant with Jesus. The synchronicity in this miracle moment is in the meeting of the angelic and the human, the male and the female, the immortal and the mortal, the transpersonal and the personal, the finite and the infinite, virginity and maternity, Self and ego. In this event, we are touched by the zeal of the divine to enter our human condition, the enthusiasm of Gabriel to announce and brighten it, and the joy of human nature to participate in it. We see the willingness of Mary to lay aside her own limited beliefs to receive ego-transcending wisdom. She will become an advocate for and a companion of all humans for the rest of history. Ultimately this scene is an indispensable compendium of wisdom since it encourages us in living and shows us exactly how to be born. The Annunciation is a metaphor. The figures in it and the event it portrays are not to be taken literally. They are archetypal images of powers and potentials within us. As Jung says: *"The incarnation of Christ is the prototype of what is being continually wrought in us by the Holy Spirit."*

Dreamwork means conscious imagination to amplify the unconscious messages of dreams. Dreams want to find expression or completion in our waking world. Active imagination is a way of doing this. Dreamwork is the synchronicity of unconscious message and conscious work. It is a way of expanding upon the themes and images in our dreams by dialoguing with them. This process honors the transcendent function of the psyche to unite and synthesize conscious and unconscious realms within us. The psyche channels images from the soul treasury within/beyond us. It is personally in us and archetypally beyond us. The psyche presents in dreams and in active imagination precisely the image that is required here and now for our rise in consciousness. This is the essence of the synchronicity of dreams: letting the light through so we can see in the dark.

Dreamwork is active imagination: engaging in a dialogue with an image or figure from a dream. "Imagination acts by impressing the stamp of humanity — of human feeling — on inanimate or merely natural objects," says Coleridge. I let this image take me where *it* wants to go, no matter how outrageous the trip. The hero goes with the flow of events with a sense of wonder. The end of wonder is the end of the journey. A fully developed experience or change is not possible in a dream. A conscious elaboration is required and it takes work, dreamwork: active imagination in the day about the night's dream.

Active imagination (described below) is like alchemy: attention is paid even to the lowliest elements and their transformation follows. Active imagination makes an accommodation with our predicament, thereby negotiating a path through it. Active imagination is not simply a technique to observe the unconscious. In it the ego asserts itself and helps our unconscious see how its demands can or cannot match the conditions of reality. Dialogue helps us relate to the figures in our unconscious rather than be possessed by them, stand in awe of them, or be frightened by them. Images are immensely responsive to the compliment of contemplation. They are enlivened and animated by it. This is how the active imagination expands and completes an image.

"Make the night joint laborer with the day," says Hamlet. Dreams initiate and further our work on ourselves. Dreamwork is our way of picking it up from there. Dante recognized this during his three nights and three days in Purgatory. Each night he had a dream which he contemplated during the day. His dreams while unconscious were all part of the work of purification he was experiencing consciously. We are being freed and freeing ourselves from ego to become the wholeness we were always meant to be, night and day. Active imagination is the daylight contribution we make to match the psyche's nightly contribution in dreams. There is optimistic synchronicity in that joint venture.

 **PRACTICE**

Consider your dream from each of the following three perspectives:

- *Intrapersonally:* all the figures of your dream are parts of your inner world

- *Interpersonally:* your dream shows your way of relating to others

- *Transpersonally:* your dream tells you about your spiritual life and destiny

Amplify your dream by using this version of active imagination:

1. Empty your mind of left-brain or distracting thoughts, using these affirmations: "I let go of ordinary thinking and analyzing. I am open to the voice that wants to come through to me." "Empty" also means empty of fear and attachment, i.e., empty of ego.

2. Look at the image, noticing the "felt sense" of it: As I hold this image, what do I feel and where do I feel it in my body? Which of the seven chakras (energy centers) is this image most comfortable in: Survival, Sex, Power, Heartfulness, Release of free speech, Wisdom, Spiritual Power?

Steps 3–6 are done in writing:

3. Dialogue with (and become) the image. Add the phrase: "This is part of myself" to an image or, "And this is my life (or body)" to a scene. Make associations until you reach an "Aha!" — the best sign of finding your personal meaning in a dream.

4. Choose nine words from all you have written to create a poem.

5. Ask for a gift or message.

6. Create an affirmation that declares the message or central point.

7. Perform a ritual that enacts the message, including thanks for it.

Dreams point to a higher potential health, not simply past crises, . . . giving clues to the archetypes of the psyche pressing for recognition.   — Joseph Campbell

Chapter Six

SYNCHRONICITY SUMMONS US TO SPIRITUALITY

The more we become conscious of ourselves through self-knowledge, and act accordingly, the more the layer of the personal unconscious will be diminished. In this way, there arises a consciousness no longer imprisoned in petty personal interests. This widened consciousness...is a function of our relationship to the world,...bringing the individual into an absolute binding and indissoluble communion with the universe....There is no individuation on Everest.

—Carl Jung

Spiritual work does not begin with action but with centered attentiveness to the messages of our inner Self in synchronicity, dreams, and intuitions. "Our unconscious manifests an intensive readiness to communicate its contents to consciousness," wrote Jung. The messages may be about choices and transitions that further our journey to individuation. Later the work becomes an engagement in a program of compassion and effective responsiveness to the needs of the world. Every pain and grief I meet is an address to me to enter the desperation of those who may not be able to find "the mysterious pass through the apparently impenetrable mountains." The desperate dislocation that occurs corresponds to the dismemberment of the hero/redeemer — a metaphor of the divesting of ego — for the sake of suffering humanity. In medieval alchemy, the torture of Jesus was in fact seen as a symbol of the prime matter being transformed into the philosopher's stone. Our gold of wholeness appears in the crucible of our own griefs and those of the woeful world. Letting go of ego is meant to be the threshold to compassion.

Compassion is not an ideal but a phenomenon of higher consciousness, the new consolidation of ego-I with Self-world. Its purpose is to reorganize the ego around all-embracing love. This is how the ego becomes spiritually coherent — as it becomes psychologically coherent by being loved. Compassion does not mean noticing pain or even understanding it empathically. Empathy is the mirroring of the pain in others. Compassion activates our empathy; it does something about it. Yet true compassion is non-deliberate and automatic too. It is like the moon which makes no specific decision to reflect itself in the pond. It simply lets it happen without planning or parceling.

Deepening Our Compassion

Take aim at my bare soul, O keen-eyed archer, Compassion.
Continually sting me, bees that know how to draw honey
From my, ah, now opening heart.

The Dalai Lamas are believed to be incarnations of Avalokitesvara, the Buddha of compassion. The Buddha is depicted with many heads to see suffering humankind from every direction. He has a thousand arms to reach out everywhere and an eye in the palm of each hand, since compassion is not blind. This is a metaphor of the spontaneous urge toward compassion flowing from the wisdom in our letting go of dualism. Once we are all one and not separate, we are all responsible for one another. Avalokitesvara, the Bodhisattva of compassion, presents the doctrine of non-duality and of the emptiness of ego in the Heart Sutra, not in Sariputra, the Bodhisattva of intellectual knowledge. The wisdom of the compassion of the awakened heart (Bodhicitta) motivates enlightened persons to give up liberation for themselves alone in favor of the liberation of others. Tara, the Mother of all Buddhas and the female aspect of compassion, was formed from a teardrop of Avalokitesvara. She vowed to help him free all of us from the fetters of fear and grasping. The Blissful Goddess is at work now as you read these words with the wish to let that happen! Buddha himself is said to be born from compassion. He also lives to show compassion and to show it reliably and universally. This is why we "take refuge in the Buddha."

Compassion is a state of mind flowing from the realization of emptiness, i.e., no inherent, self-sustaining existence in any thing or person. We are all interdependent both between ourselves and between us and all of nature. Awareness of this profound, primal, and indestructible unity leads us to mutual reverence and caring love. This is one way the wisdom of non-duality connects us to compassion.*

Compassion also flows from egolessness: "I am not in this world just for myself but just in time for others too." This is because they — and we — need assisting forces. No one person can do it, or be it, all by herself. I can afford to give this way because I have the rich gift of knowing that service is my true path. Without egolessness, I might try to proselytize or force others to follow my way. In the tonglen meditation practice of Mahayana Buddhism, one sends peace to others in exchange for their distress. This practice consists of sitting in meditation for a half hour with the realization of ego emptiness and egoless compassion. Then for ten minutes, one breathes in the dark cloud of the suffering of others and breathes forth healing opalescent light from one's own heart. The dark cloud diffuses into noth-

---

*"The wisdom realizing emptiness directly undermines the ignorance conceiving inherent existence, and the extinguishment of that ignorance in the sphere of reality is called liberation. . . . The emptiness in which all afflictive emotions have been extinguished through the force of antidotal wisdom is the true cessation that is liberation" (Dalai Lama, *The Meaning of Life from a Buddhist Perspective* [Boston: Wisdom, 1992], 64–65).

ing as it enters the no-thing of one's egoless state. It has no hook to attach itself to. One does this with the image of those one loves and then of those one does not love, and finally of those one hates.

Compassion begins with equanimity in the face of all that humans do. Once we perceive the ultimate oneness of all beings, a solidarity results between us and them. This is our capacity to love without fear. This is the fearlessness that reckons every event and encounter in life as happening at just the right time and in just the right way for us to learn what it takes to live out our destiny. In such a synchronous world, nothing can go wrong, at least not for long. In such a spiritual world, we keep finding exactly the discarded pieces of ourselves that clamor for reattachment to our psyche. This is how synchronous meetings and experiences impel us to wholeness.

How does this fearlessness happen? A compassionate act shatters the walls that divide us and reveals the touching similarities that make us no longer fear one another. *The unconditional love, immortal wisdom, and healing power of the Self are not then seen any longer as virtues we achieve but as natural consequences of spiritual liberation.* Now personal liberation is equated with liberation of all beings, since there is no separate I anyway.

A great deal of work on ourselves is accomplished by compassion toward others. "An enlightened person does not have to know much. He has the whole teaching in the palm of his hand when he has learned compassion," says the Sutra of Avalokitesvara. Intuition is the something in us that knows the whole teaching. Lively energy is the something in us that handles things. Compassion is the something in us that gives willingly and sanely. These are reliable powers that coalesce in personal integration.

Compassion is sympathetic love for those who still fear what we have learned to trust. This is expressed beautifully in the Tibetan Buddhist affirmation: "I live through the sunset of fear and desire and greet the dawn of sane love and of exuberant compassion. I will always remain loyal to those who are lost in the ever-setting sun of fear and desire." This is being true to love lived now. Buddha's message is about the utterly disappointing emptiness of the ego and the utterly hopeful compassion for those who have not yet found that out, i.e., for those who are still lost in the sunset world of fear and craving.

Wisdom is not a body of truth. It is a state of being in which truth becomes accessible within us and active through us. The big mind beyond ego looks more and more like light. As we access our powers, our body becomes less a mule to carry us or a pedestal for our ego or brain to rest on. Our body and all things are composed of condensed light, continually moving, beating musically, always already united by undying, unborn/reborn love. "Things are losing their hardness. Even my body now lets the light through," says Virginia Woolf.

An image arises to help us here. Cathedrals are human-made symbols of our entry into the fullness of our destiny of human/ divine power. They are sacred spaces that combine the multi-colored light from the stained glass with the sensuous smell of incense, music of the organ and choir, and thousands of glorious art images. This sympathy of sound and sight transports us to the world beyond these appearances. That is precisely the excursion on which we receive the light that then shines through us.

Spiritual life aims at transcendence of limitations that result from attachment to individualized consciousness. Myths and symbols are meant to show us this. They are not products of an author's mind but an ongoing collective project of humankind to work out the human conundrum. They survive because each new generation recognizes their value. Our journey is from anonymous cosmic creation to intuitive re-creation in tangible personal existence. A symbol of this in Hinduism is the gander, who represents liberation and spirituality: he swims in and skims over the water but is not bound to it like a fish. He flies between earth and heaven and so joins them together. This is a metaphor for our ability to be set free from our bondage to the events of daily life. Gander in Sanskrit is Hamsa: Ham means *I* and Sa means *this: I am this*. Ham is a Yogic sound on the exhale, Sa on the inhale: the inner gander sings his name in Yogic breathing. I am not to be confused with the mortal man who has my name and who accepts as real the habits of attachment to fear and craving, the division of opposites, and the linear view of time and of cause/effect, etc. That man is under the spell of endless projections of his passions. With every breath I say: "This am I, I am breath, the space, the all that is."

"I bring forth the universe from my essence and I abide in the cycle of time that dissolves it," the Sutra says. There is only one essence-being: the enlightened mind. It becomes humanly realized when fear and craving are seen for what they are: opposites that the ego refuses to unite, products of our ignorance. This ignorance is how the ego tries to avoid the true essence of itself and things, i.e., void. But the absolute is both void and plenitude once I can really see. Void means void of limit. (This is why the Self is void.) It is nothing and everything, a fertile void: the source and destination of all life's energy. This is why matter can neither be created nor destroyed: it is no-thing. Meditating on this leads to a realization of the identity of the individual and the universal Self. Mortal and immortal are in one envelope. The transient is a ray of the everlasting light. This is the twofold appearance of the onefold universe/Self we inhabit.

I do not know what your destiny will be, but one thing I do know: the only ones among you who will be really happy are those who have sought and found how to serve.

— Albert Schwietzer

Without being stirred from the depths by compassion, the high resolve in which you take on the burden of freeing beings from suffering cannot be induced.   — Dalai Lama

PRACTICE

• Do little favors each day for friends and then for strangers too. Never call attention to what you have done for them. If you begin to feel a sense of obligation or compulsion in this practice, discontinue it. Begin again when you can do it with choice and generosity. Most of us have habituated ourselves to misleading information about our capacity for love. It is infinitely vaster than we ever dare imagine. Little acts of love are the best way into the treasury.

In Zen, we are invited to choose the path "that heavenly presences cannot see to lay flowers upon nor demons can enviously spy upon." Buddha himself said: "When your path is secret even from gods, angels, or human beings, you are truly priestly." Can I pledge allegiance to that potential in myself by beginning in such a humble way: doing favors? Can I drop the ego and "me first" as the motivating forces behind my behavior and choices and instead present a winsomely humble and kindly love:

> *Then you have done a braver thing*
> *Than all the Worthies did;*
> *And a braver thence will spring.*
> *Which is, to keep that hid.*
>
> — John Donne

• One effective way to bring meditation into action is to carry out this resolve: "For every grace I receive, I give something of myself to others." A transformation has happened when I have gone beyond handling things, i.e., helping myself. I am now working for higher stakes: healing the world. An equation has occurred between my work on myself and my commitment to my fellow humans. This means I am spiritual.

• Here are some Hindu and Buddhist quotations that may serve as points for meditation on some of the profounder aspects of compassion:

Even by voidness, if one is devoid of compassion,
The superior path will not be found.   —Saraha

As long as just one being
Remains unliberated anywhere,
Even if I have found perfect enlightenment
I will take his place.
                    —Shantideva, *Entering the Bodhisattva's Path*

Working for others, once you have let go of ego-
    centeredness,
is the best way to achieve your own goal.

Having seen the reality as it is
Bodhisattvas have transcended birth and death,
But out of compassion, they voluntarily take on
Birth, aging, sickness, and death.

Solitary Buddhahood is the final obstacle to enlighten-
    ment.

May I attain the station of Omniscient Conqueror
To fulfill the needs of beings to the limits of space.

I beam happiness to all beings north, south, east, west.

                    —Sakya Pandita, *Illuminations*

A Spirituality of Lovingkindness

A human being is part of a whole called by us, universe, a
part limited in time and space. He experiences himself, his
thoughts and feelings as something separate from the rest,
a kind of optical delusion of his consciousness. This optical
delusion is a prison for us, restricting us to our personal de-
sires and affections for a few persons nearest to us. Now our
task must be to free ourselves from this prison by widening

our circle of compassion to embrace all living creatures and
the whole of nature in its beauty.   —Albert Einstein

The Dalai Lama says, "All beings are always kind." This is because they keep awarding us every opportunity to practice letting
go and to show humble, i.e., ego-dismantling, love. Bodhisattva
literally means enlightened warrior, i.e., one who is already
enlightened but still dedicated to the enlightenment of others.
Metaphorically, the Bodhisattva is an inner force in all of us that
is stirred by the spectacle of human suffering and meets it with
fearless love. In fact, the force *is* fearless love. The Bodhisattva
vow is: "Whatever be the highest perfection of the human mind,
may I realize it for the benefit of all the living." Once there is
no separate ego, there is no personal liberation, only a universal one. What gives the Bodhisattva strength? It is her capacity
to see the true nature of things, to bear with circumstances without fear, and to meet all situations with wisdom and compassion.
These are not virtues but simply the outcomes of love. Moreover,
they are precisely the elements of mindfulness. Is mindfulness then
perhaps a program for activating the force of fearless love?

> *If the elephant of my mind is firmly bound*
> *By the rope of mindfulness*
> *All fears will cease and virtues will become easy.…*
> *I am ever dwelling in the presence*
> *Of all the Buddhas and Bodhisattvas*
> *Who are always sharing*
> *Their unobstructed vision.*
>   —*Bodhisattva's Way of Life*

PRACTICE

Follow the path to the Three Excellences of the Bod-hisattva:

- Prior to an activity: form an altruistic intention to bring enlightenment to others.

- During the activity: realize that you, your action, and your goal are ultimately empty of inherent existence, in the sense of a separate and autonomous existence, but rather are interdependent. The ego and all its pomps are ways we have of entertaining ourselves, inflating ourselves, or scaring ourselves. Fear and craving, the sports of the ego, are meant to fill a space that seems like a void. Actually, deep down, we are pure spaciousness that is an eternal Self. This is another sense in which we are synchronicity.

- Upon completion of the activity: dedicate its value to the welfare of people and nature and to the increase of love in the world.

We establish a compassionate program when we apply the above three practices to our work, projects, and enterprises.

The Bodhisattva path is the altruistic mind of enlightenment, now operating automatically and spontaneously in daily actions. One's personal enlightenment is now secondary, a means to the goal of bringing others to enlightenment. Bodhisattvas see others' suffering and pledge themselves to their release from it in the same instant. They expend as much effort as if they could single-handedly relieve them of their suffering. Thereafter, even receiving the appreciation of others is done for their sake!

Affirmations can also induce love: repeat them until your love becomes spontaneous, universal, and continuous:

- I am becoming ever more engaged in loving service.

- The whole purpose of my life is to put everything I do into the channel of universal love.

- I am now at work for the harmony and reconciliation of all beings.

- I consecrate myself to non-violence in the face of every conflict.

- I am committed to making world peace, one person at a time.

- May I be stirred by the pain I see and make a loving response to it.

- I live through the sunset of fear and desire. I greet the dawn of sane love and of exuberant compassion. I will always remain loyal to those who are lost in the ever-setting sun of fear and desire. I am true to love lived now.

Practice this love not from a neurotic need to care-take (a compulsion), but from a serene and sane enthusiasm for fellow humans. It works best with specific individuals, not people in general. Extend love especially to people with whom you have a karmic connection, since they are the ones most helped by your love. "I cannot do this" can be reframed as: "Now I know how to do this and I am acting as if I were already fully enlightened." Remember to include all of nature in your love, showing what St. Bonaventure calls "a courtesy toward things."

Love is the best antidote to fear. The more love you have and show, the less fearful you are. Paradoxically, you increase your love within when you aim it outward. Also, your altruistic cherishing of others brings you to enlightenment faster than any method you may find. As you see yourself acting with more love and integrity, you think more highly of yourself and your self-esteem grows exponentially. This is an example of how spiri-

tual work produces a psychological benefit. Paradox: you cherish
others more than yourself and thereby cherish yourself more.

Jesus said something very touching: "O Jerusalem, Jerusalem,
how often would I have gathered you up as a hen gathers her
chicks...but you refused." Not everyone will accept the love we
offer. Then compassion means stepping back and letting go, until
things change. *Can I go on loving anyway?*

The Concrete Road of Love

It is now becoming clearer that all spirituality has one and only
one purpose: to increase our love. It is shown in engaged and tangible ways: feeding the hungry, clothing the naked, sheltering the
homeless, responding to human need. It is also a feeling response
to human needs: compassion to the afflicted, comfort to the grieving, forgiveness of injury, redressing injustice. This fits with the
Bodhisattva "four means to help others": to give what is needed,
to speak gently, to console and guide, and to be an example of
active love.

Martin Luther King gave a sermon on the disciples' asking
of Jesus if they could sit on his right and left side in the new
kingdom. They construed the kingdom to be about ego: making
sure they would get what they were entitled to. King points out
that those special places are reserved for the people who feed the
hungry, clothe the naked, etc. This is a perfect summary of spirituality: letting go of ego and showing love concretely. Toward
the end of his sermon, Martin Luther King says: "Every once in
a while I think of my death and I wonder how I will be remembered. I hope my eulogist won't mention my Nobel Peace Prize,
my education, my other awards....I want to be remembered as
one who tried to love somebody. Let him say: Martin Luther King
tried to feed the hungry, to clothe the naked, to visit the imprisoned, to help the blind see and the deaf hear....I have nothing to
leave you, no riches, no luxury. All I leave behind is a committed

life. Jesus, I don't want to be on your right or left side because of fame but because of love."

Spirituality is just such an engaged and committed life. It grants us hope: the conviction that behind the appearance of this latest victory of evil is the ultimate and lasting victory of goodness. Our hope persists not because injustices have finally ended but because they are not final. They are not final because we are not returning evil for evil and thus perpetuating it. They are not final because we are still here bringing restoring love and reconciliation. A seventeenth-century Japanese poem says: "If you keep one green bough in your heart, someday a singing bird will visit you." *What makes this believable is how happy I feel about the good thing I did today for someone in need.*

The word "nemesis" means a source of harm or ruin, one's downfall. In ancient Greece, Nemesis was revered as the goddess/personification of retributive justice. Her second name is Adrastreia, which means "inescapable." In Homer her name means "due enactment." When Tyche, goddess of luck and windfalls, bestowed fortune on someone, Nemesis, goddess of downfalls, stepped in to humble him if he arrogantly boasted (ego inflation), refused to sacrifice to the gods in thanksgiving, i.e., denied the element of grace in his good fortune, or did not use part of his wealth to alleviate the poverty of others. This is a colorful way of declaring that the touch of grace was historically associated with letting go of ego, acknowledging grace, and having the instinct to give.

One can transcend ego only by selfless service and generosity. The psyche in which ego has been dissolved wants to give away the wonderful gifts that it has found. (All our gifts were received, so giving is always passing on to others what was given to us!) Compassion is not enjoined upon us but flows naturally when we wake up to our oneness with all humanity and let go of our ego. Sages and Bodhisattvas recommended compassion *because they noticed it happening in themselves.* This is how compassion became part of the spiritual program. Why should we take others' suffering on ourselves? It *happens* when we become more spiritually conscious. Something fearlessly generous in us wants to share itself with those who have less.

Notice also how the three criteria that Nemesis looks for are precisely the foundation principles of spirituality: transcendence of ego, appreciation of grace, and compassion for others. All through the ages, in every tradition, we see this same expansive threefold sense of human potential and destiny. Buddhists affirm that when Bodhisattvas and saints catch a glimpse of us loving in this way — no matter how secretly we do it — they hasten to our side to assist and encourage us. The guardian angel metaphor points to the assisting force of grace. Love attracts grace; ego repels it.

> *After Christ's appearance, it became clear that the highest development of personality must attain to that point where man annihilates his own "I," surrenders it completely to all and everyone without division or reserve.... And this is the greatest happiness.... This is Christ's paradise.*
>
> —Fyodor Dostoevsky

 PRACTICE

• Try any one of these once each day in a simple way: Demonstrate your love for specific people in some concrete way. Find a community program that helps you feed the hungry, clothe the naked, shelter the homeless, care for those in physical need. Offer a feeling response to the emotional needs of people in your life: compassion for the afflicted, comfort for the grieving, forgiveness of injury.

The Sermon on the Mount (Matt. 5) is the Christian recipe for the dismantling of the arrogant, self-centered ego. It proposes non-violent techniques as ways of showing love. Read it as if it were meant to be taken literally and then imagine what your life would be like if you did so. Take one example of a current conflict with someone and apply Jesus' recommendations. Notice how you feel about yourself. What happens to you when you no longer care about winning, being right, or retaliating? How have you thereby found a sector of your inner Self that was perhaps unexplored before? *Is the Sermon on the Mount perhaps a portrait of us at our best—what we would look like if we were not afraid of love?*

• The Greek word for sin is *hamartia,* which literally means missing the target. Our human target is love, wisdom, and healing. Sin is a deliberate choice against those three powers. It is any act that overrides our spiritual instinct for wholeness and thus makes us miss out on the target of our destiny. Inherent in sin is an alienation from others. This loss of communion is the penalty built into sin. Write an inventory of the ways you have hurt people or cheated them or betrayed them. Write the same kind of inventory for yourself: how have you hurt or betrayed or abandoned yourself in choices you have made or in habits you have maintained? Look for compassion for yourself, not blame, and compassion for others, not disregard. Make amends to yourself and others by admitting your wrongs, asking pardon, making specific amends for the losses and pain you have caused and resolving to change your life so that you do not continue in the old way. The sight of you showing contrition, amendment, and resolution may disarm the other and free that person to forgive you, i.e., let go of blaming or hating you.

• How have I been an afflicting force in others' lives?

I may have been offensive in words, both said or neglected to be said, or in actions, both done and left undone. Some of these transgressions are known only to me and some are felt by and known to others. Look back over your life and list your important choices, decisions, and milestones. What indirect ripple effects of pain have any of these had on others? What deliberate choices have I made that have been abusive, led to hurt, or caused a loss? What agreements have I broken? How have I acted *in spite of fear* and thereby grown more courageous? How have I acted (or failed to act) *because* of fear and thereby lost access to my courage? How have I acted with an arrogant or entitled ego?

Apply this same model to yourself. How have you hurt yourself or let others hurt you? What is the best chance love can have to work in your life from now on? *Use each of the points in the above model now in reverse: How have I been an assisting force in others' lives?*

Ready for Birth

Man does not change at death into his immortal part, but is mortal and immortal even in life, being both ego and Self.

—Carl Jung

Synchronicity is the keystone of the arch of psychological and spiritual integration. It is up to us to see it and to be it. We see synchronicity when we go beyond the limits of our linear mind and our clinging ego. We are synchronicity when we say yes to the world that opens beyond ego: the kingdom within. Spirituality is a grace that enlivens and enriches our efforts to dismantle our narcissistic ego's fear and grasping so that we can say yes unconditionally to the conditions of human existence, show universal love to human beings anywhere, and live in respectful harmony with nature everywhere. We human beings have a knack for reaching beyond our given limits. Our capacity for transcendence makes it possible for us to become aware of this power higher than our own ego. (Such a Higher Power is, of course, the source of the capacity!) Synchronicity manifests this power.

"Initiation is a death to something which is ready to be surpassed....Initiation is passing by way of symbolic death and resurrection from ignorance and immaturity to the spiritual age of an adult," writes Mircea Eliade. Spiritual initiation adopts the same symbolism as is seen in madness and chaos: dissolution of order. This is a metaphor for the dissolution of the profane ego, the ego without a Self. The eschatological symbol of this is the "end of the world." The after-life, in this context, may mean: there is a continuity in Self-consciousness. No such promise is made to the grasping ego.

Synchronicity comes into play when a new world/personality is ready for birth precisely as an initiatory death is undergone. The painful initiatory rites are stages of mystical death and rebirth and endow the psychic traveler with a new sensitivity to others. This sensitivity also means an ability to integrate and transform pain in oneself. Through this sensitivity the spiritual synchronously manifests itself. This is another way that compassion shows itself to be spiritually fruitful. Then you are "born into an existence which, while it is lived to all appearances in this world of ours, is framed in other existential dimensions," adds Mircea Eliade.

The Zen term for meditation is *Foo So,* which means "unproduced." Happiness is unproduced since all it takes is assent to my here and now, loving what is. The paradox of the hero's journey is the ultimate synchronicity: it is found when it is no longer sought. The confident samurai confronts us here: he no longer has to fight; he is happy to be only an amused witness. When I stop seeking, I find the here and now. I land on reality. I have compassion for it, take responsibility for it, and move through it to what comes next. Here and now is the only reality available without seeking. Seeking is what diverts me from it. Desire blinded me to the joyous lark called Now singing to me Here. When desire for otherwise disappears, happiness appears.

 PRACTICE

• In one month and again in three months, ask yourself how your finding and reading of this book was an example of synchronicity in your life. Write about it in your journal and tell one or more persons about it, verbally and in letters.

• Look at the sections of this book that you have made note of or underlined. Read them onto a tape and listen to the tape once each day for as many days as you choose. Do the same with the quotations that are scattered throughout the text. They fit the material in the book and are thus examples of synchronicity.

• If you are on line, set up or search for a chat room of other people who are reading this book. Discuss your ideas and your progress with the practices with them. Share ideas about the practices you have thought of on your own to supplement or substitute for those I have offered.

• Dedicate the work you have done in this book/journey to the welfare of the world, offering all your more lively love, your new knowledge, and your healing powers to the treasury of wisdom from which all we wanderers can draw. We are always reinvesting our graces and progress in the vast treasury of human evolution. A good affirmation is: "When I achieve, I share." Decide and declare that whenever you achieve an advance in love or wisdom, you extend it to all your fellow humans that they might progress in the same ways. "Whenever and in whatever I expand, I extend."

• When you feel truly happy, remember to say: "May all beings feel this happiness with me." This engenders a view of happiness as a gift you have received in order to give it away. Happiness is then not a personal possession but a bond with all humankind. When you are sad or discouraged, remember that many other people the world over are feeling what you are feeling at the same time. Join with them: "May all those feeling what I am feeling find a way through it. May they be helped by my work on myself. May I be helped by theirs."

• Read the following affirmations onto the same tape. If one stands out, use that one repeatedly throughout the day. Change any of them to suit your own needs, timing, and position on the path:

I am thankful for the work I have accomplished and the graces I have received in the reading and working of this book.

I acknowledge and appreciate the synchronicities in my daily life.

I acknowledge a meaning in every chaos.

I acknowledge a world beyond my senses, a truth beyond my intellect, a wisdom beyond logic, a power beyond my limits, a serene design despite any distressing display.

I am thankful for the graces that take me beyond my limits.

I seek community with others on my path.

I embrace the givens of life: beginnings and endings, aloneness, change, unfairness, unpredictability, and sometimes being given more than I can handle.

I say yes unconditionally to what is.

I open myself to every transformation that is ready to happen in and through me.

I respect the right of others to question or reject my path.

I reclaim my body as a channel of spirituality: I celebrate my powers and passions.

I drop the need for certainty; I am comfortable with ambiguity.

I let go of fear and obligation and live by love and choice.

I keep finding an inner source of strength and comfort in and beyond my soul.

I disperse compassion and love wherever I go.

I consecrate myself to join with others to end war and injustice in my lifetime.

I keep finding new companions on my journey to sanctity.

I redeem the earth and include all humanity in my heart.

My only search is for that which is always and already all of ours.

I am thankful for the synchronicity that led me to this book!

For all that has been: Thanks!
For all that will be: Yes!
— Dag Hammarskjöld

• King Bimbisara gave the Buddha a bamboo grove near Raja-graha to be used as a personal retreat. Picture it as you imagine it to be and go there now in your heart. The human heart is, after all, the bamboo grove, the retreat in which you can be silent and unseen for a while and from which you emerge to be articulate and eminently visible, when the time for that comes.

How to Stay and See

Stand stable here
And silent be....
Here at the small field's ending, pause....
— W. H. Auden

In this final section, we pull together some of the more salient ideas of the book and show how they can work for us.

We are aware of our psychological needs — attention, accep-tance, affection, and allowing. Some of our spiritual needs have become evident in the course of these pages: initiatory experi-ences in which our task may be to feel pain, let go of ego, and show compassion, grace in which our task is simply to receive, intuitions and synchronicities that point to or confirm a path for us, validation by someone who confirms our path and supports us, i.e., spiritual mirroring.

As the fulfillment of psychological needs results in a coherent sense of identity, the fulfillment of spiritual needs results in a grateful sense of wholeness. Identity is something we work for; wholeness is who and what we always and already are. Spiritual needs lead to a realization and manifestation of wholeness, not to the creation of it. Psychological work takes effort and will power. Spiritual practice takes responsiveness to grace (forces that assist us in transcending our limited will and intellectual powers) and willingness to pronounce the unconditional yes to that which is. This means accepting the things about life that do not change, i.e., the conditions of our existence in the human community: suffering, unfairness, impermanence, aloneness.

Psychological work begins with acknowledging the issue that faces us. We then can address, process, and resolve it. What is the spiritual way of handling what comes up in our lives? It may begin with looking for ground as in the distinction between figure and ground. In the *Mona Lisa*, the woman is figure and the background (with the river, etc.) is ground. As long as I look at the figure, I miss the ground. An issue or conflict that faces me in life is figure; what is the ground? It must be something unnoticed, invisible. In fact, behind all appearances is a reality that is invisible to the eye. Wordsworth refers to the sudden synchronous: "flash of the mystery of the invisible world." The whole reality is figure *and* ground. So wholeness is what we miss when we see in our habitual ways. I see even less when I am obsessed with any one person or thing. This is the real danger in fear and desire. Francis Thompson expresses it this way:

> *The angels keep their ancient places*
> *Turn but a stone and start a wing!*
> *'Tis ye, 'tis your estranged faces*
> *That miss the many-splendored thing!*

To stay is to stay with what is, responsive to its changes. To stay in this way means staying without controlling, desiring, fearing, expecting. *To see* is to release ourselves from obsession with our predicament, to enter the space behind the appearances, the ground behind the figure. To stay and see is the synchronicity of mindfulness.

I do not see the whole picture when I focus on one thing, i.e., when I am caught up in a compelling drama or in a rigid interpretation of it. How can I contact the ground, the greater perspective? I need more than focused attention if I am to see fully. A diffuse attention is necessary, i.e., attentiveness, presence, mindfulness. The Sanskrit word for mindfulness actually comes from two words meaning attend and stay. To accomplish this is to let go of our habitual ways of seeing, including evaluating, judging, fearing, desiring, attaching to outcome. Simply to sit in the space around our reality is mindfulness in it. This is meditation on our present moment rather than control of it.

Our psychological work is to address, process, and resolve our conflicts. A spiritual approach to our conflicts balances this work with a legitimate *breather* for dropping out of the drama, a recess from the struggle, a release from dualism. Instead of continually focusing on the conflict, we take a break. We let our drama fade from view for the moment and concentrate instead on the space around it. This is the pause we keep referring to throughout this book. It is the pause in music, unheard but essential for the pleasing flow of the rhythm. As long as I am caught up in dramatic storylines of fear or desire, I fail to hear the rich spiritual rhythms in my life. Mindfulness opens me to a wider context in my story beyond the content of it. The content is psychological (figure); the context is spiritual (ground). Our work will always be in both areas. Then we do not "miss the many-splendored thing." Some further examples of the two perspectives are listed in the chart on the following page.

Every psychological crisis is a loss of something we were holding on to. Around and within this loss is its ground, its space. This space is the power to let go. Since spirituality is letting go, it is the ground of our psychological work. This is exactly how psychology and spirituality are integrated. It also explains why spirituality is not disembodied from our story but the fuller dimension of it.

In the ground of each of our experiences is a vast potential for its fuller realization or even its opposite. Behind ego is egolessness; behind fear is fearlessness. When I become overly attached to one, the other is occluded. When I let go of my grip on one, the other appears more luminously. Behind the figure of intimacy

FIGURE	GROUND
Conscious	Unconscious
Ego	Self
Persona	Shadow
False Self	True Self
Thought	Imagination
Logic	Intuition
Words	Silence
Cause/Effect	Synchronicity
Dreams	Archetypes
Female energy	Male energy
Fear	Excitement
Desire	Plenitude
Transitions	Heroic journey
Psychological work	Spirituality
Holding on	Letting go
"I"	Universe

between two people is the connectedness among all sentient beings. Behind the betrayals and abuses I survived in childhood is a fortitude and strength that was ever-building in me and is accessible to me now in whatever I have to face. Behind abandonment is the space that has opened up for me, a space in which I am free to move in new ways. When I feel abandoned, I lose the sense of space as open. It closes in on me as isolation, i.e., I am abandoning my own ground, my own wholeness. This sense of ground, of a larger orbit for my existence, is spiritual attentiveness.

We never have to invent a space; it is everywhere. Around a figure there is space. Between figures there is space. Around my abandonment feelings there is space, unattended to, unappreciated. Between my broken relationships in the course of my life, a space wanted to open. Perhaps I never noticed it or entered it because I filled it with some new relationship.

Space, or ground, is what makes something more than what it appears to be, more than we fear it is. I am more than meets the eye and so is everything else. I and everything are therefore whole: figure and ground, visible and invisible, psychological and spiritual. This is another way of accounting for the unity of all beings, all equally arising from the deathless pure open ground of existence, the void over which the Spirit brooded on the day of creation.

This space is also referred to in Zen as *shunyata,* the void. It may be feared by the frantic ego as a sterile void or a black hole. Actually, it is a fecund void because it offers us the fuller dimensions of any reality. Such a spacious void is the ground that underlies wholeness: a limitless openness. It grants us, finally, what nothing else can: room to move. Is this what we ultimately fear: the room to move on? Is this why we keep heaven closed till after death? "I saw Heaven open" (Apoc. 19). *Dare we glimpse it now?* That heaven is the space in our hearts that lets the love through "and makes one little room an everywhere," as John Donne says.

 ## PRACTICE

How do we work in the ground-space of our story? The first and most powerful way is mindfulness, the technique we know and use daily. Here is another exercise:

Write a sentence (using one of the models below) about your present personal crisis or issue. Use a piece of typing paper, horizontally, and write in the center of it: Either...or. If...then. Because...I. Here are examples of the sentences: Either I stay in control, or everything will fall apart. Either I stay with you unhappily, or I leave you unwillingly. If they find out, then I lose my job (or reputation, etc.) Because you left me, I intend to punish you.

Draw a box around each of the two clauses with the comma unboxed in the center. Study your sentence with its boxes, the space between them and around them. The boxes are the figure and the space is the ground. See if your eye can reverse figure and ground for a few seconds so that the space becomes something.

| Either I stay in control | , | or everything will fall apart |

Look steadily at the comma. A comma in speech represents a pause. A pause is to the ear what space is to the eye. This comma has created a space: ENTER HERE AND PAUSE. Breathe regularly and deeply as you do this, paying attention to each in-breath and each out-breath and the little space between each breath.

Allow yourself to be with your statement with the pause button pressed on all judgments, fears, desires, attachments to outcomes. Experience your statement with clarity and pure awareness, with no layers of drama around it, only space around it. Simply stay in the space and attend to breathing there. This part may take the rest of the day — or of your life — and what better way could there be of spending it?

Notice the content of the sentence. Do you see a sense of necessity in it? The second part seems forced to follow from the first? This is a dualism. It makes the sentence a "sentence" of a judge. Who is that judge? Do not attempt to integrate or combine the clauses of your statement. Instead, find an alternative that does not give in to either side of the dilemma. Notice that this cannot be done. You are stumped! "Stumped" is the left brain's response to space.

Being stumped makes us feel powerless. This is why we fear space. What are we fearing? We are fearing the gap that has opened in our heretofore reliable logical categories. We are fear-

ing the space that undermines logic and underlies every reality —
"the field beyond right and wrong," "heaven open," "the mysterious pass." Continue simply to attend and stay. It will all yield; it
will change. The gap will become an opening, the Taoist "mysterious pass" will appear in the apparently impenetrable mountains
before you. This is the *pause* that restores. Make no attempt to
figure anything out. Simply breathe, letting go of the need to
know anything and paying attention to the space.

*Here is what happened to the original sentences after this
process:*

"Either I stay in control . . . " became: "I let the chips fall where
they may." I am not caught in having to control (a form of pain)
or in being the victim of chaos (not an adult option). I dropped
into the space, fell into the gap, and there I found a way to live
that releases me from the dilemma, is still responsible, and is
much more realistic. (When I myself did this exercise with this
as my chosen statement, I laughed out loud when the "chips"
sentence came to me. Humor is the ground of all our dramas!)

"Either I stay with you unhappily, . . . " becomes: "We work together on changing things." "If they find out . . . " becomes: "I will
be the one to tell and will tell it proudly or with willingness to
make amends and be done with it." I am released from shame,
the opposite of being mirrored. Now I can mirror myself. "Because you left me . . . " becomes "I let go of the need to punish
you. I grieve your going and get on with my life." I am free of
vengeance and open to compassion.

The new statements were there all along within the originals,
in the space, the comma-pause. Each of them confers a power.
Each new version is what your situation looked like before your
ego got hold of it. The good witch said to Dorothy, "You've had
the power all along! Just click your heels. . . . " Her power was the
ground under her, the ground of power was under her illusory
figural belief that she was powerless.

What actually happened in the movement from the figure to
the ground of our story? We stripped our ego of judgments, fears,

desires, and attachments, and entered the mindful state in which the ego's knowledge is unnecessary. We did not know how to fix things, so we chose to know even less. There is a poem by St. John of the Cross which begins with that same paradox: "I entered I knew not where and there I stood not knowing: nothing left to know.... " We did what Rembrandt did one day in his father's windmill: see a space in reflected light but see it as a form. This is the Zen realization that "form is emptiness and emptiness form." Once this has happened to us even once, there is no going back to imprisonment in our dramas and our habitual reactions to them. There is space and spacious perspective.

To contact this soul space, not filled in by drama, is to find the fruit of our mindfulness meditation: direct perception of one's reality without the ego's embroideries of fear, desire, expectation, attachment to outcome, wish, judgment, shame, blame. This means seeing the headline and not the editorial. When we drop attachment to outcome, a gap opens in the ego's cycle of fear and craving. Surrender results. "I observe my life as a silent and fair witness who feels all feelings deeply but is not overwhelmed by any one of them." Usually, the story is the figure; the silence is the ground. In mindfulness, these are reversed. Our silent soul becomes the focus, the duck blind out of which we see the world flying by, but with no intent to catch it, only satisfaction in seeing it at last with equanimity and amusement.

We will still have a story, but not one we have to tell. We will still have fears, but not ones that stop us. We will still have desires, but not ones that blind us. We will, in fact, have "ever more perfect eyes in a world in which there is always more to see," as Teilhard de Chardin says. Our spiritual capacity may never be large enough to accommodate all the light that shines on us — no more than our capacity to exult in the days of our children's infancy ever lasted long enough to contain all the joy they beamed upon us.

• *Slow down now as you read this paragraph and contemplate the connections it presents:* Celtic spirituality has a fascination with the sacred realm of the *between:* the place or moment in which the veils between the physical and spiritual worlds are so thin that we easily cross over. The between is the threshold as a beach is between the land and the ocean or adolescence is between childhood and adulthood. This mysterious between-world has appeared in every chapter of this book: soul is between ego and Self, synchronicity between cause and chance, mirroring between I and Thou, dreamwork between unconscious and conscious, poetry between prose and wordless communication, destiny between effort and grace, love between letting go and going on, our practices between learning and doing. This same between is the transcendent function of the psyche that produces the healing third when we honor opposites. By synchronicity, every moment stands on the threshold between time and eternity — and lets us stand there too.

• I look back over my life and all that has happened. I recall the people I have known and all they did to me or for me and all that I did to or for them. I begin with my parents and end with the most recent person I have met: I see how it has been like a story; an order and a continuity pervades it. I affirm a trust that it has a meaning. Love makes meaning visible. I trust its power. With love as my only defense, I am invincible. Now:

I contemplate my lifeline with each of its turning points.

I notice the messages that limited or expanded me (Don't go, don't go that far).

I see the afflicting and assisting forces: mortal and immortal, those who encouraged or repressed my lively energy.

I recall my griefs and how they were mourned, my gifts and how they were given.

Where was my effort and where was grace?

What were my breakthrough events of destiny and awakening?

Which crises and relationships were initiatory?

Which places or jobs opened me to new dimensions in myself?

Where were the opportunities to develop and release my gifts to the world?

How did I say yes or no?

How did I befriend or deny my shadow: my dark, ego-inflated side and the bright, untapped potential in my Self?

If I believe that the way everything turns out after I have done all I can to fix or change things reveals my path, what is my path right now?

I picture this scene: all the characters on my life's stage take a bow: villains and heroes become equal in this moment. All were necessary to the plot and the denouement; all were entertaining!

I greet each with compassion and thanks, realizing that *this is what it took for me to become who I am.* Now what?

I am empowered, i.e., I can do the practices without further instruction.

I have opened a door for you that no one can close.

—Apocalypse 3:8

EPILOGUE

We are put on earth a little while, that we may learn to bear the beams of love.
　　　　　　　　　　　　　　　　　　　　—William Blake

The purpose of synchronicity is to release the riches of the spiritual Self.

By a combination of effort and grace, these riches empower me to share unconditional love, universal wisdom, and healing powers and allow me to find freedom from fear and attachment, which is the enlightenment of me, and freedom for giving and receiving, which is love of you.

The final practice is a life of love.

To love is to enter the ultimate and most perfect synchronicity of all.

In love, the most striking of all coincidences occurs: two hearts match in their encounter and enfolding of each other. Each grants the very tenderness the other wanted all her life to find or waited all his life to find again.

Love is the only bridge that hearts can toss across the yawning void of emptiness that the mind will make. It is the only fire on earth that can melt the ego in an instant.

Love forgives every offense with exactly the brand of healing that makes new offenses unlikely. It reaches beyond "I and Thou" to all living beings in far-flung compassion and unconditional caring.

Love lets go, never losing what is has once held.

Love lives on, never ending what it has begun.

Love remains steadfast, never abandoning what it has cherished.

Love is the coincidental rendezvous of closing and opening, of kneading and rising, of hungering and banqueting, of halting and dancing, of living and dying.

The universe does not have a heart. It is one. It beats in the waves and in these breezes that caress the willows. It beats in my heart now with an unceasing rhythm always harmonizing with yours.

In fact, in love there is neither yours nor mine but only everyone's yes.

About the author

David Richo, Ph.D., is a psychotherapist, teacher, and writer in Santa Barbara, California, who combines Jungian, transpersonal, and mythic perspectives in his work. His previous books are *How to Be an Adult: A Handbook on Psychological and Spiritual Integration* and *When Love Meets Fear: How to Become Defense-Less and Resource-Full.*

Dr. Richo gives lectures and workshops nationally. Some of these are on audio cassette. A CD-ROM, *Dreams and Destiny,* based on the chapter on dreams in this book, is also available.

For a catalog of tapes, send a legal-size, stamped, self-addressed envelope to U.M., Box 31027, Santa Barbara, CA 93130. Please state an interest in the CD-ROM if you also want information on that.

OF RELATED INTEREST

Ann Tremaine Linthorst
SOUL-KISSED
The Experience of Bliss in Everyday Life

"Speaks to the intellect as well as to the heart. It is almost a how-to book
for seeing with the soul. I placed it on my reference shelf as a reminder
to change my perspective. I recommend it to customers who feel
that the solutions to their problems are eluding them.
The response has been positive." —*New Age Retailer*

0-8245-1492-0; $ 15.95

Paula D'Arcy
GIFT OF THE RED BIRD
A Spiritual Encounter

When Paula D'Arcy lost her husband and baby in a car crash, she began
an inner search for a faith that was stronger than fear. In *Gift of the Red
Bird* she shares her remarkable spiritual adventure: Paula literally
journeyed alone into the wilderness for three days, allowing the Creator
to speak through that creation. As she surrendered to the power of God
alone, a red bird appeared and, without words, began to teach . . .

0-8245-1590-0; $ 14.95

Please support your local bookstore, or call 1-800-395-0690.
For a free catalog, please write us at
THE CROSSROAD PUBLISHING COMPANY
370 LEXINGTON AVENUE, NEW YORK, NY 10017

We hope you enjoyed Unexpected Miracles. *Thank you for reading it.*